The Rastafari Movement

A Beginner's Guide

Nicholas Mwangi

Daraja Press

Published by Daraja Press
https://darajapress.com
Wakefield, Quebec, Canada

ISBN 9781990263873

Cover and interior design: Kate McDonnell

Library and Archives Canada Cataloguing in Publication

Title: The Rastafarianism : a beginners guide / Nicholas Mwangi.
Names: Mwangi, Nicholas, author.
Description: Includes bibliographical references.
Identifiers: Canadiana 20230526500 | ISBN 9781990263873 (softcover)
Subjects: LCSH: Rastafari movement.
Classification: LCC BL2532.R37 M83 2023 | DDC 299.6/76—dc23

CHAPTER 7 – Rituals and Practices

CHAPTER 8 – Rastafari religious and philosophical literature

CHAPTER 9 – Conclusion

Preface

Rastafarianism is a complex movement interwoven with elements of social movement, Pan-Africanism, Afrocentrism, philosophy, and religion. However, this intricate movement defies conventional classification of religion or a movement, lacking a centralized structure and instead encompassing a multitude of historical backgrounds, groups, and branches.

The complexity of Rastafarianism is illuminated by its various adherents, each embracing distinct belief systems and structures often requiring in-depth research on its philosophy and history; nevertheless, there exist fundamental assumptions, tenets, and goals that unite and bind all Rastafarians.[1]

Numerous academic studies have examined various aspects of Rastafarianism, resulting in seminal works such as *The Rastafarians* (1997), *Chanting Down Babylon: The Rastafari Reader* (1998), and *Rastafari: from Outcasts to Culture Bearers* (2003). These scholarly endeavors, spearheaded by scholars such as Leonard Barrett, Nathaniel Samuel Murrell, and Ennis Barrington Edmonds, have paved the way for a substantial body of literature on the subject. Yet, amid this comprehensive body of work, Rastafari: A Beginner's Guide distinguishes itself not as another exhaustive academic pursuit, but rather as a simple primer intended for both seasoned Rastafarians and importantly, for new readers with little to no prior knowledge of the Rastafari movement.

Rastafarianism's global perception often rests upon stereotypes and sensationalized practices—misunderstood reggae music, cannabis use, and distinctive dreadlocks. While many Rastafarians do indeed sport dreadlocks and incorporate marijuana into their spiritual rituals, the essence of the Rastafari lifestyle transcends these attributes. A prevailing misconception has thus ensnared Rastafarianism, perpetuating a flawed narrative that has led to global discrimination against its adherents.

With legendary musicians like Bob Marley, Black Uhuru, and Wailing Souls proudly promoting the Rastafari message in their music and taking pride in Haile Selassie and Marcus Garvey, spreading its message across the globe and attracting millions of followers of different nationalities and races, the

---

1 Bedasse, M. A. (2017). *Jah Kingdom: Rastafarians, Tanzania, and Pan-Africanism in the Age of Decolonization.* Chapel Hill, The University of North Carolina Press

popularity of reggae music ushered in the quick rise of the Rastafari movement outside of Jamaica.

Rastafarianism's embrace of cultural preservation, vegetarianism, and Pan-Africanism has garnered widespread recognition and respect. However, its status as a relatively new movement in comparison to established religions and philosophical institutions has rendered it vulnerable to scrutiny and skepticism. Even though Rastas are opposed to being labeled with – "isms" because Rastafarianism is more than religion, it is a way of life.

Dreadlocks, a distinctive symbol of Rastafarianism, have sparked contentious issues, with female students in African schools encountering adversity due to their adherence to this practice. Notably, in Kenya. It was a topic of national discussion which involved the intervention of the High Court. The Kenya High Court recognized Rastafari as a religion and culture on 13 June 2019, citing Article 30 (1) of the Constitution, which stipulates that everyone has the right to freedom of conscience, religion, thinking, belief, and opinion. This milestone highlighted the growing imperative to honor freedom of conscience, religion, and belief, heralding a new chapter in the movement's evolution.

The stereotypes against Rastafarians are also a result of their origins in Jamaican ghettoes, where they were politically active, and their association with the poor masses. This has altered over time as the movement evolved it extended to the professionals and the middle class, fostering a more inclusive and diverse community.

Its historical trajectory, foundational values, way of life, and the ethical complexities it grapples with are all covered in this beginner's handbook.

Human Rights

The rights to freedom of conscience, religion, and belief as stipulated in the United Nations declarations and in the African Charter on Humans and Peoples.

United Nations Universal Declaration of Human Rights

Article 18

Everyone has the right to freedom of thought, conscience and religion; this right includes freedom to change his religion or belief, and freedom, either alone or in community with others and in public or private, to manifest his religion or belief in teaching, practice, worship and observance.

United Nations Declaration on the Elimination of All Forms of Intolerance and of Discrimination Based on Religion or Belief

Article 2

No one shall be subject to discrimination by any State, institution, group of persons, or person on the grounds of religion or belief.

Article 4

All States shall take effective measures to prevent and eliminate discrimination on the grounds of religion or belief in the recognition, exercise and enjoyment of human rights and fundamental freedoms in all fields of civil, economic, political, social and cultural life.

African Charter on Human and Peoples Rights

Article 8

Freedom of conscience, the profession and free practice of religion shall be guaranteed. No one may, subject to law and order, be submitted to measures restricting the exercise of these freedoms.

CHAPTER 1

Background

Rastafari has extended from a small and formerly undesirable cult into a dominant force which influences all levels of national life; and it has done so against formidable odds, political harassment and general condemnation. The Rastafari has dramatized the question that has always been uncomfortable in Caribbean history, and the question is where you stand in relation to blackness.[2]

In his commentary on the Rastafari, George Lamming joined the ranks of those members of the Caribbean community who correctly noted that the Rastafari movement carried with it a certain continuity from the days of slavery, a continuity of resistance and confrontation with white racism. The Rastafari movement, in all its contemporary manifestations, challenges not only the Caribbean but the entire Western World to come to terms with the history of slavery, the reality of white racism and the permanent thrust for dignity and self-respect by black people. The racial consciousness which was stamped yesterday in the Universal Negro Improvement Association, and which is today encrusted in the locks and beards of the Rastafari, stands as a potent force in the struggle for justice.

Race consciousness remains an integral part of the class consciousness of African peoples as long as Euro-American culture seeks to harmonise the economic and political domination of black peoples with attempts at destroying their cultural personality. Such a harmonizing project of dehumanization started in the era of the slave trade, when the day-to-day atrocities were unified by a cultural assault—whether French, Dutch, Spanish, Portuguese or British—to impose European ideas and values on the dominated Africans.

In the face of cultural resistance—manifest in religious practices, the preservation of African languages, African medicinal and healing crafts, and musical forms of communication—and open slave revolts, the slavers deepened their racist theories, building upon the original biblical justification for racial inferiority with the kind of pseudo-science which led to the theories of Arthur Jensen (that black people were genetically inferior to white people).[3]

---

2 See Campbell, H. (1987, page 1). *Rasta and Resistance*. New Jersey, Africa World Press, Inc.
3 ibid.

Rastafarianism is a multifaceted movement, thus it defies singular definition. Some scholars categorize it as an emerging religious movement, while others view it as a social movement as it originated in the 1930s among poor and socially disadvantaged Afro-Jamaican people. Both analogies are true; the Rastafari movement has historically been associated with political struggles and Pan-Africanism anywhere it has spread to, due to its fervent opposition to colonization, systemic oppression, and the prevailing order of "Babylon" (Global North). Pan-Africanism and Rastafarianism are interconnected movements that emerged in the 20th century, both with roots in Africa and the African diaspora. Additionally, its historical development and philosophical foundations connect it to a monotheistic organization that worships a single God known as Jah, the movement's monotheistic deity, Rastafarianism draws inspiration from Psalms 68:4: "Sing unto God, sing praises to his name: extol him that rideth upon the heavens by his name Jah, and rejoice before him."[4] Jah represents more than a spiritual entity; it encapsulates the interconnectedness of humanity, the African diaspora, and the divine. The movement's theological underpinnings underscore the unity of all people, a vital tenet in its struggle against oppression and societal divisions.

The Rastafari movement first appeared in Jamaica in the 1930s following the coronation of Ras Thafari Makonnenas, better known by his name upon leadership, Haile Selassie I (meaning "Power of the Trinity"). The crowning of Haile Selassie as emperor of Ethiopia was the catalyst that brought to the fore the deep-seated attitudes of many Afro-Jamaicans toward Jamaica's colonial establishment. It also heightened their desire for liberation from oppression and alienation. The Rastafarian movement, therefore, emerged because some Afro-Jamaicans perceived the crowning of an African monarch as the sign of their liberation from colonial oppression. Haile Selassie's ascension to the throne of Ethiopia was more than a mere event; it symbolized hope, liberation, and a resurgence of Afrocentric pride. The movement's early adherents perceived this event as a sign of imminent emancipation from colonial oppression. Anchored in their conviction that Haile Selassie embodied the divine power of the Trinity.

Further, Emperor Haile Selassie's historic visit on 21 April 1966 legitimized the movement on an international stage, galvanizing a global community of Rastafarians. This period also saw the emergence of iconic figures like Bob Marley

---

4 Edmonds, E. B. (2002). *Rastafari: From Outcasts to Culture Bearers*. New York, Oxford University Press

and Peter Tosh, whose reggae music became a powerful platform for disseminating the Rastafari message. Marley's influence transcended borders, making Rastafarianism synonymous with reggae music.

Nevertheless, Rastafari's philosophy and foundation dates back to a time before Haile Selassie and Bob Marley. it is essential to acknowledge the foundational figures who laid the groundwork for its growth. Marcus Garvey, revered as a prophet, and Leonard Howell, known as the first Rasta in Jamaica, alongside other pioneers like Joseph Hibbert, Archibald Dunkley, and Robert Hinds, contributed to shaping Rastafarianism's ethos and principles.

Marcus Garvey

Marcus Garvey was born in Jamaica on August 17, 1887. An activist, orator, and visionary leader who left an indelible mark on the fight against racism, inequality, and injustice during the early 20th century. Garvey emerged as a steadfast advocate for the rights and pride of black people worldwide. His legacy is deeply intertwined with his passionate pursuit of returning to Africa as a means of liberation and empowerment for black people. Through his organization, the Universal Negro Improvement Association (UNIA). Key to Garvey's philosophy was the belief in Africa as the ancestral home and rightful place of belonging for black people. The trauma of slavery and forced displacement had severed countless ties to the African continent, and Garvey recognized the imperative of reconnecting with this historical heritage. The UNIA became a platform through which Garvey rallied millions of followers, often referred to as Garveyites, who shared his vision of cultural pride, economic self-sufficiency, and the recognition of Africa's central role in their history. Garvey's eloquence and charisma as a speaker were pivotal in garnering support for his cause. Drawing upon religious references, particularly from the Bible, he articulated a message of self-liberation and mental emancipation. His powerful statement

> We are going to emancipate ourselves from mental slavery, for though others may free the body, none but ourselves can free the mind. Mind is our only ruler sovereign.[5]

highlighted the essence of his mission. He recognized that freedom extended beyond physical liberation; it encompassed a psychological liberation from the shackles of inferiority instilled by generations of oppression.

However, when the confrontation with Jamaican authorities grew more serious and culminated in his incarceration in London for alleged fraud, the momentum of the UNIA movement began to wane in the 1930s. After serving five years in prison, he was sent back to Jamaica; at that point of his release, UNIA was no longer vibrant. Despite this setback, Garvey's principles endured, and his teachings continued to resonate through the efforts of other activists. One such figure was Leonard Howell, a former UNIA member, who propagated Garvey's ideas, particularly the prophetic words that foretold the crowning of a black king in Africa. Garvey had said to his followers:

> Look to Africa, when a black king shall be crowned, for the day of deliverance is at hand.[6]

This is thought to have occurred in 1930, when Ras Tafari Makonnen was crowned the new Emperor of Ethiopia and became known as Emperor Haile Selassie. Another facet of Garvey's philosophy was his proclamation about the divine. He rejected the notion of a God defined by the white man's perspective, advocating instead for a God rooted in Ethiopia's heritage. His words, "Whilst our God has no color, yet it is human to see everything through one's own spectacles"[7] conveyed the idea that spirituality could be experienced and

5 Autodidacy 17. (31 August 2017). *Marcus Mosiah Garvey: Emancipate your African mind!* New York Amsterdam News. https://amsterdamnews.com/ news/2017/08/31/marcus-mosiah-garvey-emancipate-your-african-mind

6 Black History Month 2023. (2008). *Haile Selassie – King, God or Redeemer?* [online] Available at: https://www.blackhistorymonth.org.uk/article/section/bhm-he%20roes/haile-selassie-king-god-or-redeemer/ [Accessed 27 Sept. 2023]

7 Garvey, M. M. (1986). *Philosophy and Opinions of Marcus Garvey.* USA, Majority Press

understood through diverse cultural lenses. Garvey's conviction in the God of Ethiopia as the universal deity for black people reinforced his message of cultural pride and self-determination.

Leonard Howell and the Evolution of Rastafarianism

Leonard Howell, a Garveyite and Black Nationalist, stands as a remarkable figure in the history of Jamaica and the global Rastafarian movement. He continued the fight for the poor and vulnerable in Jamaica after the decline of UNIA, but he gradually shifted away from preaching Garveyism; it was Howell who proclaimed Haile Selassie's divinity, which became his main mobilizing focus. Out of admiration for Selassie, he founded the King of Kings Mission and proclaimed himself Selassie's ambassador in Jamaica. He also wrote the first book on Rastafarianism, *The Promised Key*. The book is one of numerous kinds of literature which Rastas read. Notably, Howell's teachings deviated significantly from orthodox Christianity. He rejected the notion of a white Jesus Christ and propagated the belief that Selassie embodied the reincarnation of the black Messiah. This unorthodox interpretation posited Selassie as the fulfillment of biblical prophecies and the catalyst for black liberation not only in Jamaica but worldwide. In 1933, he drafted six Rastafari movement convictions, that included:

1. Hatred for the White race.
2. The complete superiority of the Black race.
3. Revenge on Whites for their wickedness.
4. The negation, persecution, and humiliation of the government and legal bodies of Jamaica
5. Preparation to go back to Africa and
6. Acknowledging Emperor Haile Selassie as the Supreme Being and only ruler of Black people.[8]

However, as Howell's teachings gained traction, they also faced vehement opposition from government authorities and the broader society. The unapologetic proclamations of racial superiority and animosity towards the white race drew scrutiny and led to the movement being labeled as a cult or gang. This antagonism culminated in numerous arrests and persecutions, casting a shadow on the movement's growth. Most of those ideas are no longer followed by Rastafari adherents worldwide as it has evolved to extend beyond Howell's original teachings.

---

8 Coursehero.com. (2023). Available at: https://www.coursehero.com/file/23635170/Rafarianism [Accessed 27 Sept. 2023].

Leonard Howell

In 1940, Howell established the Pinnacle, the first Rastafarian village in Jamaica, as a self-sufficient community. This marked a significant step towards the practical realization of Howell's ideals within a communal framework. Yet, even as Rastafarian communities flourished, they continued to face persecution from Jamaican police. The infamous Coral Gardens incident of 1963 stands as a tragic testament to the tensions between Rastafarian communities and the wider society, leading to a violent clash resulting in eight deaths in the commune, injuries, and over 150 arrests.

The enduring pressures endured by Rastafarians over the years, coupled with a comprehensive investigation by Public Defender Arlene Harrison Henry, led to a moment of reckoning for the Jamaican state. The report's findings, including the haunting events of Coral Gardens, prompted a call for reparations and an official apology to the Rastafarian community. In 2017, Prime Minister Andrew Holness publicly apologized on behalf of the Jamaican government, acknowledging the pain and suffering endured by Rastafarians.[9]

While Howell's ideas sparked persecutions and clashes, his legacy paved the way for a broader understanding of Rastafarianism that extended beyond his original convictions. The movement's evolution serves as a testament to the resilience of a movement that continues to navigate its complex relationship with history, society, and spirituality.

9 Bedasse, op.cit.

Rastafarianism as a Resilient Social Movement

The word Rastafari is often followed by "movement." If the Rastafari, however, remain a social movement, they must be among the most long-lived.[10] The Rastafari movement has captivated social movement scholars with how it has evolved over time and found ways to renew its activism through the years that includes intellectuals in the twenty-first century, considering that social movements have a propensity to fizzle out quickly.

Essentially, social movements typically emerge around shared grievances or issues that resonate with a group of people. These grievances could be related to inequality, injustice, discrimination, lack of representation and human rights violations. Those who define Rastafari as a social movement point out that it emerged in a context of colonialism and racial discrimination, with many of its early followers being descendants of African slaves in Jamaica. The movement's rejection of Eurocentric standards and its emphasis on African identity and pride were inherently political statements against colonial oppression and racism and that it was also influenced by the ideas of Marcus Garvey, who advocated for the empowerment and repatriation of Black people to Africa. Garvey's "Back-to-Africa" movement resonated with Rastafarians, as they also believed in the importance of returning to their African roots and rejecting the cultural and societal norms imposed by colonial powers.

As Prince (2009) puts it, the chaotic and complex nature of the evolution of new peoples and social movements involves surprises—events that change substantially the evolutionary trajectory of a group. We can never know when their experience, their story, will shift radically to another script, perhaps overlaying, conjoining, the narratives that already exist. The Rastafari survived the ridicule and suppression of the 1930s and 1940s, greatly increased their membership and influence between 1955 and the mid-1970s, moved beyond the devastating impact of Henry's twin debacles and the Coral Gardens incident and the crackdowns that followed to still exists as a formidable movement.[11]

Even in contemporary times, Rastafari continues to stand against social injustices on multiple fronts. The movement's global reach allows it to engage in

---

10 Bedasse, op.cit..
11 Prince, C. (2009). *Becoming Rasta: Origins of Rastafari Identity in Jamaica.* NYU Press.

issues such as racial profiling, police brutality, and systemic racism, which resonate with the experiences of Black individuals and communities worldwide. Rastafarians have been active participants in protests and advocacy efforts, demanding justice and equality.

Henry's "twin debacles" and the Coral Gardens incident were undoubtedly significant challenges that tested the resilience of the Rastafari movement. Yet, these challenges did not lead to its demise. Instead, the movement weathered these storms and emerged even more formidable. This ability to adapt, overcome, and sustain its momentum continues to be seen today and demonstrates the depth of its commitment to its core principles.

CHAPTER 2

Rastafarianism and Other Religions

Rastafarianism is frequently compared with other major world religions such as Christianity, Buddhism, Hinduism, and Islam. This comparison arises from the recognition that Rastafarianism constitutes a spiritual and religious belief system characterized by its distinctive teachings, practices, and cultural components. These comparative assessments serve the purpose of elucidating both the commonalities and distinctions between Rastafarianism and other religious traditions, as well as situating Rastafarianism within the broader framework of religious diversity. This chapter will look briefly at the similarities while acknowledging the differences, without delving into an exhaustive analysis of the latter.

Rastafarianism and Christianity

These two religious movements bear both similarities and stark differences. While proponents of comparison draw attention to shared elements such as monotheism, the concept of a messiah figure, and reverence for sacred texts, a deeper examination unveils the distinctive beliefs, practices, and historical contexts that set these two movements apart. Nevertheless, proponents who compare Rastafari to Christianity point out that monotheism stands as a fundamental cornerstone that bridges the gap between Rastafarianism and Christianity. Both traditions espouse the belief in a single, omnipotent God. Christianity articulates this through the concept of the Holy Trinity, acknowledging God as encompassing the Father, Son (Jesus Christ), and the Holy Spirit. On the other hand, Rastafarianism places paramount significance of the deity Jah, an embodiment of the divine force that governs the universe.

Second, the concept of a messiah figure is a pivotal theme in both Rastafarianism and Christianity. In Christianity, Jesus Christ is hailed as the divine Messiah who descended to Earth to redeem humanity from sin. Conversely, Rastafarianism identifies Emperor Haile Selassie I of Ethiopia as the messiah, revered under the title "Ras Tafari." This association between Selassie and the messianic figure stems from the prophetic belief that he would lead the oppressed African diaspora to liberation and restore their dignity. The parallel drawn between Jesus Christ and Haile Selassie accentuates the human desire for salvation and hope, manifesting through distinct historical narratives.

An additional point of convergence emerges from the reverence attributed to sacred scriptures. Christians hold the Bible as their holy text, a compendium of spiritual wisdom and moral guidelines. Similarly, Rastafarians hold certain texts, notably the "Holy Piby," in high esteem, often interpreting biblical passages in ways that resonate with their socio-cultural context. This shared affinity for sacred texts show the role of scripture as a source of guidance, inspiration, and cultural identity for these religious communities.

Despite these points of similarity, Rastafarianism and Christianity are distinguished by their unique beliefs, practices, and historical trajectories. Rastafarianism, born out of the social and political conditions of Jamaica in the early 20th century, evolved as a response to the colonial and racial oppression faced by African descendants. The movement sought to reclaim African heritage, challenge societal norms, and cultivate a distinct identity rooted in the veneration of Emperor Haile Selassie as a messianic figure. In contrast, Christianity boasts ancient origins, with its roots stretching back to the time of Jesus Christ in the Middle East. Over centuries, Christianity has metamorphosed into diverse denominations and spread across the globe, assuming a plethora of cultural and theological forms.

Rastafarianism and Christianity share notable parallels in their beliefs about monotheism, messiah figures, and reverence for sacred texts. However, the distinct contexts in which these two movements emerged, coupled with their unique theological tenets, practices, and historical narratives, underscore their individuality.

Rastafarianism and Islam

There are those who have pointed out on the shared tenets between Rastafarianism and Islam on their unique beliefs, historical origins, and cultural practices. There exist remarkable points of convergence that highlight the universality of certain human values such as community and brotherhood, respect for prophets, and spiritual practices. Nevertheless, there are not the same in any manner and there exists major differences.

Both Rastafarianism and Islam emphasize the significance of community and brotherhood among their followers. In Islam, the Ummah, or the global Muslim community, is not merely a geographical or cultural concept; it is a unifying force that transcends borders and ethnicities. Muslims are urged to support and care for one another, embodying the principle of brotherhood.[12] Similarly, within the framework of Rastafarianism, a strong emphasis is placed on the collective experience of oppression and the shared cultural heritage. This shared history serves as a foundation for a sense of community that fosters resilience and unity. While their historical narratives differ, both Rastafarianism and Islam acknowledge the power of community in shaping the lives of their adherents.

Respect for prophets is another striking parallel between these two faiths. Rastafarianism venerates figures such as Haile Selassie I, who is seen as a spiritual leader and guide, and Marcus Garvey as a prophet. In Islam, profound reverence is reserved for the Prophet Muhammad, a central figure whose teachings and actions continue to inspire Muslims worldwide. Although the specific figures are distinct, the underlying principle of looking up to spiritual leaders who exemplify righteous living and offer guidance is a shared element. This reverence for prophetic figures deepens the connection between believers and their faith, motivating them to live in accordance with the values espoused by these leaders.

Spiritual practices form an integral part of both Rastafarianism and Islam, guiding the daily lives of their practitioners. Islam's Five Pillars serve as a comprehensive framework that encompasses various dimensions of faith and practice. From the declaration of faith *(shahada)* to the pilgrimage to Mecca *(hajj)*, these pillars provide a roadmap for leading a spiritually fulfilling life.[13] On the other hand, Rastafarian practices encompass a diverse range of rituals, including prayer, meditation, and the use of sacramental herbs like cannabis for worship. While the specific practices differ, the underlying purpose remains the same: to establish a deep connection with the divine, seek guidance, and cultivate inner peace.

In short, Rastafarianism and Islam are two distinct religions that bear their own theological doctrines, historical roots, and cultural expressions. However, the similarities that emerge from an examination of their values and practices are both enlightening and enriching.

---

12 www.al-islam.org. (2022). Brotherhood In Islam. [online] Available at: https://www.al-islam.org/islamic-moral-system-tafsir-commentary-surah-al-hujarat-49-jafar-subhani/brotherhood-islam

13 Encyclopedia Britannica. (n.d.). sawm | Religion, Meaning, Reasons, & Importance. [online] Available at: https://www.britannica.com/topic/sawm

Rastafarianism and Buddhism

Rastafarianism and Buddhism are two distinct religious and philosophical systems with some notable differences, but there are also a few similarities that can be drawn between them, particularly in certain aspects of their beliefs and practices such as:

Focus on inner peace and spiritual growth: Buddhism places a strong emphasis on inner peace, meditation, and spiritual development. The ultimate goal is to attain enlightenment or Nirvana through self-realization and self-improvement. Rastafarianism: Rastafarianism also encourages inner peace and spiritual growth, often through the use of meditation and prayer, which leads to a deeper connection with the divine.[14]

Rejection of materialism: Buddhism teaches the impermanence of material possessions and emphasizes the importance of detaching from worldly attachments.[15] Rastafarians often reject materialism and consumerism, focusing instead on a simpler way of life and a connection with nature.

Respect for all life: Buddhism promotes compassion and respect for all living beings, often leading to vegetarianism or veganism among its practitioners, thus there is no slaughtering of animals for human consumption. Most Rastafarians are vegetarians, and do adhere to a plant-based diet as a way to respect all forms of life.

Rastafarianism is known for its commitment to social justice and the promotion of equality. Rastafarians often advocate for the rights and well-being of marginalized groups, especially people of African descent. They have historically been involved in various social and political movements, including efforts to combat racism and colonialism. Buddhism also places a strong emphasis on compassion and social responsibility. The Buddha's teachings include principles like the Eightfold Path, which encourages ethical behavior, right livelihood, and right action.[16]

---

14 Longevity. (n.d.). *From Babylon to Nirvana: Rastafarianism vs Buddhism.* [online] Available at: https://vocal.media/longevity/from-babylon-to-nirvana-rastafarianism-vs-buddhism.
15 Daniels, V. (2020, December 11). *How Buddhism Teaches us to Un-Learn the Mindset of Materialism.* Medium. https://medium.com/mind-cafe/how-buddhism-teaches-us-to-un-learn-the-mindset-of-materialism-81e1f2b8afa2
16 Rahula, W. S. (2015). The Noble Eightfold Path: Meaning and Practice. Tricycle: *The Buddhist Review;* Tricycle. https://tricycle.org/magazine/noble-eightfold-path

Rastafarianism and Hinduism

Rastafarianism and Hinduism stand out as two distinct yet interconnected paths that have captivated many people. While they arise from different geographical and cultural backgrounds—with Rastafarianism emerging in Jamaica and Hinduism originating in India—there are intriguing parallels that suggest a subtle interaction between the two. Indeed, scholars of religion argue that, Rastafarianism's ideals, use of marijuana, and dreadlock style have been greatly influenced by Hinduism. Between 1845 and 1917 around 35,000 Indian servants were brought to Jamaica from India. The Indian laborers brought with them their religious traditions and introduced marijuana to Jamaica,[17] a plant deeply ingrained in Hindu practices for its spiritual and medicinal properties. By the time Rastafarianism emerged in the 1930s it had been influenced by the new culture of Indian immigrants.

One significant area of convergence between Rastafarianism and Hinduism lies in their emphasis on spiritual focus and connection. Both traditions encourage adherents to embark on a journey of inner exploration and cultivate a profound connection with the divine. In Hinduism, this connection is nurtured through meditation, rituals, and devotional practices aimed at unifying the individual soul *(atman)* with the ultimate reality *(brahman)*. Rastafarianism, on the other hand, directs its focus toward Jah, the spiritual essence of God, and promotes spiritual practices that foster an intimate relationship with nature as a means of connecting with the divine.

Moreover, both Rastafarianism and Hinduism employ symbolism and sacred texts to convey their teachings and beliefs. Hinduism boasts a rich array of sacred texts, such as the Vedas, Upanishads, and the Bhagavad Gita, each offering insights into spirituality and ethical living. Similarly, Rastafarianism draws inspiration from the Bible, particularly the Old Testament, which it interprets through a lens that aligns with its convictions about Ethiopia and African heritage, in addition to the Holy Piby and *Kebra Negast*.

Ethical living is another shared principle that unites these seemingly disparate traditions. In Hinduism, the concept of dharma prescribes moral duties and responsibilities that individuals must fulfill to maintain harmony in various

---

17   Burgess, V. (2007). Indian Influences on Rastafarianism *[Thesis Indian Influences on Rastafarianism]*. The Ohio State University. Department of Comparative Studies Honors Theses

aspects of life.[18] Rastafarianism echoes this sentiment by emphasizing the importance of ethical conduct, justice, and resistance against oppression. Both traditions provide a moral compass that guides their adherents towards righteous living and social responsibility.

Lastly, mutual reverence for nature and the environment further solidifies the connections between Rastafarianism and Hinduism. In Hinduism, nature is often perceived as an extension of the divine, and rituals are dedicated to honoring the interconnectedness between the natural world and the spiritual realm. Similarly, Rastafarianism's focus on the sanctity of the earth and its natural elements, their love of communal living and vegetarian diet aligns with Hinduism's perspective.

While Hinduism is confronted with the issue of the caste system Rastafarianism does not have such a system, clearly separating the two religions. The Hindu caste system traditionally consists of four main varnas or social classes: Brahmins (priests and scholars), Kshatriyas (warriors and rulers), Vaishyas (merchants and farmers), and Shudras (laborers and servants). Beyond these four varnas, there are numerous sub-castes and groups. At the bottom of the hierarchy are the Dalits, formerly known as "untouchables," who historically faced severe discrimination and social exclusion. Rastafarianism emphasizes unity, equality, and the liberation of all oppressed people regardless of class or race.

In conclusion, Rastafarianism stands as a unique and vibrant spiritual movement that has both distinct elements and intriguing intersections with other religions. Its roots in Jamaica and its emphasis on the divine significance of Emperor Haile Selassie I have fostered a strong sense of community and unity among its followers.

Rastafarianism and Liberation Theology

In the context of religion and social movements, Rastafarianism and Liberation Theology have emerged with striking similarities such as the fervent dedication to social justice and the liberation of marginalized communities. While they hail from different corners of the globe and have distinct religious beliefs, these movements share a profound commitment to dismantling systems of oppression rooted in racism, economic inequality, and the enduring scars of colonialism.

---

18 History.com Editors (2017). Hinduism. [online] History. Available at: https://www.history.com/topics/religion/hinduism

Liberation is a central theme in both Rastafarianism and Liberation Theology. Rastafarianism seeks the spiritual and cultural liberation of black people, particularly in the context of Jamaica and the broader African diaspora. The movement was born out of the historical legacy of slavery and colonialism, which left a deep impact on the psyche of African descendants. Rastafarians believe that through their faith in Haile Selassie I, they can attain spiritual liberation and reconnect with their African roots.

On the other hand, Liberation Theology emphasizes the liberation of the poor and oppressed from socio-economic and political injustices. It emerged in Latin America as a response to widespread poverty, inequality, and social injustice.[19] Liberation Theology's goal is to free people from the chains of oppression in the here and now, challenging the notion that poverty is a natural consequence of progress.[20] Both movements, in their own way, call for a radical transformation of society, driven by a commitment to justice, peace, and love.

Critiquing colonialism and its far-reaching consequences is a shared historical thread between these two movements. Rastafarianism, deeply rooted in Jamaica's colonial history and the enduring specter of slavery, sees colonialism as the source of their suffering and displacement. Their response involves asserting their African heritage and identity as a potent tool of resistance. Liberation Theology, on the other hand, often blossoms in nations marred by the exploitative machinery of colonial powers. It arises as a reaction to oppressive structures imposed by these colonial forces, structures that particularly afflict indigenous and marginalized communities. Liberation theologians argue passionately for the active involvement of the Church in dismantling these oppressive systems and forging a more just and equitable society.

Both Rastafarianism and Liberation Theology promote activism and social engagement. Rastafarians express their activism through music, art, and cultural expressions, which have served as powerful conduits for raising awareness about social injustices. Reggae music, with its resonant messages of resistance and unity, has acted as a global megaphone for the Rastafarian cause.

Proponents of Liberation Theology often engage in community organizing, advocacy, and political activism. They work tirelessly to address issues such

19 Chawane, Midas H (2014). The Rastafarian movement in South Africa: A religion or way of life? *Journal for the Study of Religion*, [online] 27(2), pp.214–237. Available at: https://www.scielo.org.za/scielo.php?script=sci_arttext&pid=S1011-76012014000200011 [Accessed 27 Sept. 2023].
20 Linden, I. (1997). Liberation Theology. CIIR

as land reform, poverty, and human rights abuses. The activism of both movements serves as a testament to their unwavering commitment to bringing about substantial change in the lives of the marginalized.

While the religious beliefs of Rastafarianism and Liberation Theology differ significantly, both movements incorporate spirituality into their quests for social justice. Rastafarianism places a strong emphasis on the divine figure of Haile Selassie I, whom they see as the messianic figure that will lead them to spiritual and cultural liberation. Spirituality serves as a source of strength and inspiration for Rastafarians in their struggle for justice.

Liberation Theology, on the other hand, integrates Christian theology and spirituality into its call for social justice. It interprets the message of Jesus Christ as a call to action, urging the Church to actively engage in addressing social and political issues. The fusion of spirituality and social justice in both movements highlights the interconnectedness of faith and the pursuit of a just society.

To sum up, both Rastafarianism and Liberation Theology cultivate a sense of cultural identity and pride within people. Rastafarianism encourages Afrocentric cultural expressions and venerates African heritage as a means of reclaiming an identity that centuries of oppression had stripped away. Similarly, Liberation Theology places a spotlight on the cultural and religious identity of oppressed groups, recognizing that these unique experiences shape their perspectives and struggles.

CHAPTER 3

Mansions/Houses

Marred by prejudice and discrimination, the Rastafari movement emerged as a beacon of hope and unity for those seeking a different path in Jamaica and inspired by African spirituality. Rastafarianism has transcended borders and attracted followers from various walks of life. It constitutes different mansions or denominations within the faith. Three of the most prominent ones are Nyabinghi, Bobo Ashanti, and Twelve Tribes of Israel. These mansions can be likened to denominations within Christianity or different schools of thought within a philosophical movement, each with its distinct identity yet united by common goals and general beliefs.

Nyabinghi

The Nyabinghi order stands as the foundational pillar among the three mansions of Rastafarianism, embodying a rich history of culture and spirituality. The Nyabinghi order is the oldest of the three mansions. The term Niyabinghi means "black victory" (niya = black, binghi = victory). It may also be spelled in a variety of other ways, such as "Nyabinghi", "Nyahbinghi", "Niyahbinghi".[21]

It is also known as the Theocratic Priesthood/Livity Order of Nyabinghi/Ethiopian Orthodox Church. It was named after Uganda's Queen Nyahbinghi. Almost all ceremonies took place after being touched by Nyabinghi's spirit. Before the elders could offer sacrifices, they discussed her spirit. She also served as a medium for communication between members of the community and God.[22]

Central to the Nyabinghi philosophy is the veneration of Haile Selassie, the embodiment of the Supreme Deity for its adherents. With Ethiopia, often referred to as Zion, serving as a symbol of sacred land, and the promise of Africa's resurgence, the Nyabinghi order paints a vivid connection of hope and faith. This belief in the imminent return of Africa to its former glory resonates powerfully within the hearts of its members, infusing them with purpose and determination.

---

21 YADA, R. (n.d.). The Incient Nyahbinghi Order: [Review of The Incient Nyahbinghi Order]. Durban, Isalem Publications

22 Fagan, C. (2021). *The history of Queen Nyabinghi, Shamanic Priestess of East Africa.* [online] AfricaOTR. Available at: https://africaotr.com/the-history-of-queen-nyabinghi-shamanic-priestess-of-east-africa/

Guided by an Assembly of Elders, the Nyabinghi culture finds expression through ceremonial gatherings and rhythmic drumming sessions known as "groundations." These gatherings are more than mere congregations; they are a testament to the spiritual connectivity among Rastafarians and their ancestral heritage. Through chants, hymns, prayers, and discussions on Rastafarian principles, the Nyabinghi members strengthen their bonds with each other and with the teachings that shape their faith. A distinctive facet of the Nyabinghi way of life is the emphasis on purity and naturalness. This often translates into dietary practices, with many adherents choosing a vegetarian or Ital diet—embracing the harmony of natural, organic sustenance. Such a lifestyle echoes their reverence for the earth and the interconnectedness of all life.

The other two mansions of Rastafarianism, the Bobo Shanti and the Twelve Tribes of Israel, trace their origins back to the Nyabinghi order. The Nyabinghi mansion serves as the bedrock from which the spiritual and philosophical branches of Rastafarianism spread, branching into different interpretations while retaining the core principles that unite them.

Bobo Ashanti

In 1958, Emanuel Charles Edwards founded the Bobo Ashanti, a Rastafari mansion that would go on to become a distinct and spiritually significant branch within the larger movement. Also known as the Ethiopian Africa Black International Congress (EABIC), the Bobo Ashanti's foundation marked a divergence from existing Rastafarian orders and the establishment of a new trinity, with Haile Selassie, Emperor of Ethiopia, as the living God, Charles Edwards himself as the spiritual leader, and Marcus Garvey as the prophet.

Emanuel Edwards' earlier activism, advocating for the rights of black individuals in Jamaica and promoting their repatriation to Africa, had already solidified his position as a dedicated advocate for change. Observing what he perceived as a weakening of the spiritual essence within the Niyabinghi order, Edwards decided to create the Bobo Ashanti as a response to the perceived dilution of spiritual principles.

Similar to other Rastafarian sects, the Bobo Ashanti view Haile Selassie I as a divine incarnation of Jah (God), embodying the essence of spiritual divinity. However, their interpretation of Rastafarian creed sets them apart from groups such as Nyabinghi and the Twelve Tribes of Israel, as the Bobo Ashanti's beliefs follow a more traditional trajectory.

The visual identity of the Bobo Ashanti is characterized by their distinctive attire. Members don long robes and tightly wrapped turbans, symbols of their adherence to religious principles and their commitment to the Rastafarian way of life. Central to their beliefs is the strict adherence to Jewish Law, a practice that encompasses the observance of the Sabbath and the promotion of race pride and reparations. Within the diverse landscape of Rastafarian mansions, the Bobo Ashanti stands out as a beacon of spiritual strength and organizational discipline. This mansion is regarded as being the most structured, organized and disciplined in comparison to the other major mansions in the Rastafari movement.[23]

Twelve Tribes of Israel

The Twelve Tribes of Israel is one of the several "mansions" or divisions within the Rastafari movement founded by Vernon Carrington also known as the prophet Gad in 1968, Kingston, Jamaica. This mansion derives its name and identity from the historical twelve tribes of Israel, a concept deeply rooted in its practices and beliefs. The Twelve Tribes of Israel mansion has evolved over time, transitioning from a centralized and disciplined house to becoming the most liberal among the Rastafari mansions, allowing its members to worship according to their individual inclinations.

One of the fundamental practices of the Twelve Tribes of Israel is the daily reading of a chapter from the Bible. Members are encouraged to complete reading the entire Bible within a span of three and a half years.[24] This practice emphasizes the importance of a strong spiritual foundation and a deep connection to biblical teachings. Additionally, the number twelve holds great significance within the mansion, drawing parallels between the twelve tribes mentioned in the Bible, the twelve disciples, and the twelve months of the year.

A distinctive feature of the Twelve Tribes of Israel mansion is the practice of assigning names and colors to its members based on their birth month and corresponding tribe. This practice adds a layer of identity and symbolism to their spiritual journey. For instance, someone born in April would be associated with the tribe of Reuben and the color silver, while a May-born individual

23 Barnett, M. (2005). The many faces of Rasta: Doctrinal Diversity within the Rastafari Movement. *Caribbean Quarterly*, 51(2), 67–78. https://www.jstor.org/stable/40654506?origin=JSTOR-pdf
24 ibid

would be linked to the tribe of Simeon and the color gold.[25] This naming tradition creates a sense of unity and shared identity among the members.

The foundation of the Twelve Tribes of Israel's belief system rests on the notion that the second coming of Jesus Christ manifested in the form of Haile Selassie, the revered Emperor of Ethiopia, whom they refer to as Jah Rastafari. This belief underscores their spiritual connection to Ethiopia and their reverence for Haile Selassie as a divine figure.

Another distinctive objective of the Twelve Tribes of Israel mansion is the pursuit of repatriation, a concept deeply ingrained in Rastafari ideology. This objective reflects a desire to return to the ancestral homeland, Africa, and serves as a manifestation of their longing for cultural and spiritual reconnection.

One of the remarkable aspects that sets the Twelve Tribes of Israel apart is its inclusive membership policy. Unlike Bobo Ashanti, this house does not adhere to racial barriers, welcoming individuals of all races and backgrounds. This inclusive approach mirrors the movement's broader emphasis on unity and equality.

Equally noteworthy is the mansion's pioneering stance on gender equality within the Rastafari movement. The Twelve Tribes of Israel has paved the way for acknowledging and promoting equal roles for men and women. This forward-looking perspective reflects a progressive interpretation of Rastafari principles (Barrett 1997).[26]

Despite their differences in practice and interpretation, all Rastafari mansions share common goals and general beliefs. They universally revere Haile Selassie I as a divine figure, emphasize the importance of African heritage and identity, advocate for the legalization of marijuana as a sacrament, and promote a message of unity, love, and peace.

It's important to note that Rastafari is a dynamic and evolving faith, and there are many other smaller mansions and independent groups within the movement. While Nyabinghi, Bobo Ashanti, and Twelve Tribes of Israel are among the most widely recognized, they represent only a portion of the movement.

25 ibid
26 ibid

Members of the Kenya Land and Freedom Army,
sometimes called Mau Mau, wearing dreadlocks

Rastafari Experiences in Kenya

The Rastafari movement, often associated with reggae music and the iconic image of dreadlocks, has found a unique presence in Kenya. Despite the absence of official statistics, Kenya has one of the largest fanbase of reggae music in Africa and has a registered Rastafarian association. Kenya is also the home of the famous liberation movement Mau Mau that is often linked to the Rastafari movement in Kenya due to its dreadlock image.

Dreadlocks, a hallmark of Rastafarian identity, are often misunderstood and sometimes mistakenly linked to the origin of Rastafarianism within the Mau Mau struggle in Kenya. However, it is important to clarify that there is no direct connection between the two. The dreadlock image within the Rastafari movement in Kenya is seen as an extension of the Mau Mau struggle, by its followers' symbolizing resistance against oppression and colonialism. This interpretation resonates with Rastafarians, who view their faith as a means of continuing the fight against historical injustices and freedom not achieved to date.

The roots of Rastafarianism in Kenya can be traced back to the establishment of two major Rastafarian orders: the 12 Tribes of Israel and Bobo Ashanti. The 12 Tribes of Israel, founded by Vernon 'Prophet Gad' Carrington in 1986, marked the beginning of the Rastafarian movement in Kenya. Subsequently, the Bobo Ashanti, officially known as the Ethiopia Africa Black International Congress (EABIC), emerged in 1992 with the arrival of Priest Richie, Priest Harry, and Priest Rackal,[27] who were the first students of the order's founder, Prince Charles Emmanuel Edwards. These pioneers arrived in Nairobi and established a "tabernacle" in Nairobi's Kayole estate before relocating to Utawala, where the EABIC Church of Black Salvation still stands active today.[28]

Rastafarianism in Kenya became a national conversation during two pivotal moments. The first occurred when a schoolgirl from a Rastafarian family was barred from attending school due to her dreadlocked appearance. This incident escalated to the high court, ultimately resulting in a landmark victory for the Rastafarian movement in Kenya. The state officially recognized Rastafarianism as a legitimate religion, sparking nationwide discussions on religious rights and freedom. Media outlets played a significant role in disseminating this news, further raising awareness about the movement.

The second occasion that brought Rastafarianism to the forefront was when the Rastafari Society of Kenya petitioned the high court to legalize the use of marijuana for spiritual purposes. This petition, though contentious, was grounded in the claim that Rastafarians were being harassed, intimidated, arrested, prosecuted, and even imprisoned for growing and using cannabis to connect with the "Almighty Creator." The movement's pursuit of religious freedom and the decriminalization of marijuana fueled passionate debates across the country.

Rastafarianism in Kenya, when combined with reggae music, has found a particularly receptive audience in the country's informal settlements. The messages of oppression, resistance, and hope inherent in Rastafarian and reggae culture resonate deeply with Kenya's youth. Providing them with a sense

27 The Star. (2020). *A glimpse into Rastafarianism in Kenya, its history.* [online] Available at: https://www.the-star.co.ke/sasa/lifestyle/2020-06-12-a-glimpse-into-rastafarianism-in-kenya-its-history/
28 www.pd.co.ke. (2020). Rastafarian movement in Kenya mourns its fallen leader – Moses Mbugua. [online] Available at: https://www.pd.co.ke/news/rastafarian-movement-in-kenya-mourns-its-fallen-leader-moses-mbugua-37673/

of identity, purpose, and community. This connection is especially vital in contemporary society, where many young people in marginalized areas face a range of challenges, including poverty, violence, and lack of opportunities. Rastafarianism offers an alternative to mainstream culture and provides a platform for self-expression and empowerment.

Through music, particularly reggae, Rastafari has reached a global audience and resonated with young people who identify with its messages of unity, resistance, and spiritual awakening. Icons like Bob Marley and Peter Tosh have played an important role in spreading Rastafarian ideals and creating a sense of belonging for youth in informal settlements.

CHAPTER 4

The Growing of Dreadlocks:
Spiritual and Cultural Significance in Rastafarianism

The Rastafarians' most striking image is their dreadlocks. Rastas grow dreadlocks in line with the Bible scripture and other philosophical beliefs.

Leviticus 21:5 and Numbers 6:5 are two key passages in the Bible that are often cited by Rastafarians to support their practice of growing and maintaining dreadlocks. Leviticus 21:5 guides against making baldness on one's head and shaving off the corner of the beard, while Numbers 6:5 emphasizes the holy significance of allowing the hair on one's head to grow as an act of separation unto the Lord. These verses serve as a foundation for Rastafarians' conviction that allowing their hair to form dreadlocks is a spiritual expression of their faith and devotion.

> All the days of the vow of his separation there shall no razor come upon his head: until the days be fulfilled, in which he separateth himself unto the lord, he shall be holy, and shall let the locks of the hair of his head grow.
>
> – Numbers 6:5

It is important to recognize that while dreadlocks are a distinctive feature of Rastafarians, not all Rastafarians grow them, and not all individuals with dreadlocks are Rastafarians. Over time, dreadlocks have transcended their religious origins and become a popular hairstyle adopted by people from diverse backgrounds for reasons that may not be linked to Rastafari.

House of Youth Black Faith

However, the history of dreadlocks within the movement is a tale of evolution and transformation, rooted in the social and cultural context of its time. While pioneers of the movement like Leonard Howell and Joseph Hibbert did not have dreadlocks, the emergence of this distinctive hairstyle can be traced back to a significant juncture in Rastafarian history—the formation of the Youth Black Faith in Trench Town during the late 1940s. The Youth Black Faith (YBF), a group of five brethren bound by their devotion to Rastafarian teachings, emerged as a radical force within the movement during the mid-20th century, comprising Brother Taf, Pete, Brother Firsop, Badaman, and Watson.[29]

---

29 Eschert, R (2023). Uvm.edu. Available at: https://www.uvm.edu/~debate/dreadlibrary/eschert.html

The YBF played a pivotal role in shaping the Rastafari movement from the late 1940s through the 1960s. At its inception, the YBF's members did not universally wear dreadlocks, but they actively encouraged their adoption. It was during this period, around 1947, that the practice of growing dreadlocks began to gain prominence among Rastafarians. Members of the Youth Black Faith encouraged locks and bearded men were even thought to be the chosen ones who would repatriate to Africa.[30]

Yet, like many aspects of the Rastafari movement, the significance of dreadlocks extends beyond the image. On an aesthetic level, dreadlocks embody a rejection of Eurocentric standards of beauty imposed by Babylon. Rastafarian's view practices like hair straightening and skin bleaching as attempts to conform to white ideals of beauty, reflecting a disconnection from one's African heritage. In contrast, dreadlocks symbolize a reclaiming of pride in African physical characteristics and a reconnection with authentic identity.[31]

One notable theory posits that Rastafari movement's adaption of dreadlocks and symbolism could have been influenced by the Mau Mau revolutionary movement that fought against British colonialism in Kenya. The use of dreadlocks as a symbol holds a prominent place in both the Youth Black Faith and the Mau Mau movement. The Mau Mau fighters in Kenya were renowned for their distinctive dreadlocked hairstyles, which not only distinguished them but also represented their resistance against British oppression. Similarly, the Youth Black Faith adopted dreadlocks as a central facet of their identity. Newspapers published across the African diaspora played a vital role in amplifying the voices of those resisting colonial rule. The dreadlocked images of Mau Mau fighters were circulated widely, serving as powerful symbols of the fight against British colonialism in Kenya. These images resonated deeply with Black communities around the world, inspiring a sense of solidarity and a shared struggle against oppression.

The journey of dreadlocks within the Rastafari movement shows the dynamic nature of cultural and religious expressions. It demonstrates how symbols can evolve over time, shaped by historical events, social contexts, and collective aspirations. While the movement's pioneering figures did not embrace this hairstyle, the Youth Black Faith's advocacy for dreadlocks contributed to their eventual adoption as a central element of Rastafarian identity.

---

30 ibid
31 Edmonds, op.cit.

The MOVE movement, founded in Philadelphia in 1972,
bombed by police in 1985.

The MOVE Movement

Over the years, one of the Move Movement images, the year of which is unclear, has circulated on social media. The image of black men and women
with dreadlocks in what appears to be a project in the United States has long
perplexed most people. The question of whether they were Rastafarians or
who exactly they are is always asked, while other false sources have portrayed
the group as a cult or terrorist organization. Its critical to understand that the
origins of the MOVE movement. It shows that people can embrace dreadlocks
image and not necessarily follow Rastafarianism. Even though, the movement
shared some elements with Rastafarianism like eating a vegetarian diet.

The Move Movement was founded by John Africa in 1972, marking the beginning of a unique chapter in American activism. It is often described as a black
liberation and back-to-nature organization. The Move members, based in West
Philadelphia, embraced a communal lifestyle like the Rastafarians but combined elements of revolutionary ideology, similar to that of the Black Panthers.
They were staunch advocates of living a life free from government interference,
police oppression, and the encroachment of technology. The group's philosophy extended to animal rights advocacy, adopting vegan diets, and embracing

homeschooling as a means to safeguard their autonomy,[32] which today some Rastas adopt.

The Move Movement's confrontations with the authorities, particularly the police, were frequent and intense. As they passionately engaged in public demonstrations against issues, they deemed important, such as racism and police brutality, they became targets for harassment and violence as a result many Move members endured physical beatings and prolonged periods of incarceration.

In 1978, a pivotal moment in the group's history unfolded when hundreds of police officers, equipped with machine guns, teargas, bulldozers, and water cannons, surrounded their property during a standoff. City authorities perceived the Move organization as a threat to the community, and tensions reached a breaking point. The siege culminated in a police shootout, during which Move members were accused of firing upon the officers, though they vehemently denied it. Tragically, a police officer named James Ramp lost his life, and several Move members sustained injuries.[33]

The fallout from the 1978 incident resulted in the arrest and imprisonment of nine Move members, known as the MOVE 9. These individuals, including Debbie Sims Africa, Janet Hollaway Africa, Janine Phillips Africa, William Phillips Africa, Delbert Africa, Michael Davis Africa, Charles Sims Africa, Edward Goodman Africa, and Merle Africa, were sentenced to serve between 30 to 100 years in prison.[34] The MOVE 9 became a symbol of resistance and the subject of an enduring campaign for their release. Then in 1985, the worse came when the Philadelphia police dropped two bombs onto the roof of the MOVE compound, resulting in the death of six MOVE members and five of their children, and destroyed 65 houses in the neighborhood.[35]

Any form of resistance especially by black people like the Move Movement is always attractive to Rastas. While both Rastafarianism and MOVE have challenged the status quo and advocated for social change in their own ways, they are separate movements with distinct ideologies, practices, and histories.

32 Contributors (2014). *Terrorists or a MOVEment? Never Forget May 13th, 1985.* [online] The Black Youth Project. Available at: https://blackyouthproject.com/terrorists-or-a-movement-never-forget-may-13th1985 [Accessed 27 Sep. 2023]

33 The Guardian. (2020). *Chuck Sims Africa freed: final jailed Move 9 member released from prison,* 7 February, Pilkington, E.

34 Demby, G. (13 May 2015). *I'm From Philly. 30 Years Later, I'm Still Trying To Make Sense Of The MOVE Bombing.* NPR.org.

35 https://content.time.com/time/magazine/article/0,9171,141842,00.htm

CHAPTER 5

Beliefs and Practices

Rastafarianism as a religious movement has distinct doctrines and practices that reflect its cultural and spiritual foundations. These practices not only strengthen the spiritual connection of Rastafarians to the divine but also contribute to the preservation of their cultural and religious identity.

InI (I-and-I)—Unity and Identity

"I&I" is a term often used in Rastafarian culture and language." This expression holds deep spiritual and philosophical implications. "I&I" is not merely a linguistic replacement for pronouns, but rather a symbol of unity and equality. Rastafarians use this term to transcend individual distinctions and emphasize a shared identity that connects every individual to each other and the divine. By replacing "you" and "we" with "I&I,". It signifies that every person, regardless of their social or cultural background, is a part of the same divine unity.[36]

Reasoning Sessions

"Reasoning sessions" are a central component of Rastafarian practices. These gatherings blend elements of collective worship, meditation, and dialogue. During reasoning sessions, participants engage in spiritual discussions about social and cultural matters. Drumming, singing, and prayers are common features of these sessions, along with the lighting of marijuana as a sacrament. The marijuana is passed among adherents as they converse, each person taking their turn. These sessions foster a sense of community and provide a platform for shared reflection and enlightenment.

Bible

The Bible plays a significant role in Rastafarian theology, much to the surprise of many. The Rastafarians' history and beliefs would be unclear without the bible. Despite their belief that Babylon, which is frequently associated with Western, white culture, has tainted the Bible's meaning over time, they embrace an enormous amount of it. The verses are interpreted by Rastafarians to mean that black people are the real Israelites and God's chosen people.

36 Bean, B. (2014). *"I-And-I Vibration": Word, Sound, and Power in Rastafari Music and Reasoning.* mdsoar.org. https://doi.org/10.13016/M2VJ4F

Different branches of Rastafarianism focus on various sections of the Bible. The Bobo Ashanti, for instance, adhere primarily to the Old Testament, using Jewish law to guide their observances. On the other hand, the Niyabinghi and the Twelve Tribes incorporate elements from the New Testament and recognize Jesus Christ. Rastafarians engage in intensive study of biblical passages, often reinterpreting narratives to reflect their history of subjugation and envision a future of liberation.

Rastas study bible passages for extended periods of time. As a way to make some biblical narratives represent the history of their subjugation, they refer to a chapter in the book of Jeremiah for instance where God identifies as a black man. They understand the Bible to promise their own freedom from exploitation and to prophesy a return to the Promised Land. They read and recite the Old Testament Bible and believe it contains their own account of their exploitation's past as well as a promise of liberation. They reject traditional Western interpretations of the Bible, which they view as having been manipulated by colonial powers to subjugate and oppress people of African descent.

They also draw parallels between passages from the Bible and events in Selassie's life, particularly his coronation in 1930 and his defiance against Italian colonial forces during the invasion of Ethiopia. Selassie himself was part of the Ethiopian Orthodox Christian faith.

Haile Selassie

On 2 November 1930, Ras Tafari Makonnen was crowned Emperor Haile Selassie I of Ethiopia. Believed to be a descendant of King Solomon and the Queen of Sheba, Selassie assumed the titles of King of Kings, Lord of Lords and the Conquering Lion of the Tribe of Judah, to some fulfilling the Biblical prophecy of a black king that had been emphasized by Garvey.[37] Several biblical texts (Rev. 5:2–5; 19:16; and 1 Tim. 4:13–14) are examples that support this belief. As the 225th heir to King Solomon and the Queen of Sheba, Haile Selassie was regarded as a representative of the Solomonic dynasty. Like many Ethiopian emperors, he referred to himself as the "Conquering Lion of the Tribe of Judah." On the Ethiopian flag, the lion was also shown with a crown and scepter. Although his status as the Messiah is a belief specific to the Rastafari movement, not all Ethiopians or people of African descent share this belief.

---

37 History.com Editors. (2018, August 21). Rastafarianism. HISTORY; A&E Television Networks. https://www.history. com/topics/religion/history-of-rastafarianism

However, the belief in Selassie's divine nature varies across different Rastafari houses or "mansions." The Bobo Ashanti, for instance, hold a particularly strong reverence for Selassie, seeing him as part of a holy trinity alongside Marcus Garvey and founder Charles Edwards, also known as "Dada Immanuel."

Prayers

Rastafarianism is a spiritual movement thus prayer is a central practice observed diligently across various houses. The movement's followers engage in reading the Old Testament, keeping the Sabbath, and engaging in prayer as part of their spiritual routine. The Bobo Ashanti, for example, pray toward the East three times a day—6 a.m., noon, and 6 p.m. Prayer is considered a means to uphold justice, peace, and harmony, and it plays a significant role in gatherings and ceremonies. Chanting, drumming, and other forms of musical expression often accompany these prayers.

Psalm 150's Lord's Prayer is an example of a prayer verse recited by Rastas.

> Praise Jah in his sanctuary;
> Praise him in his mighty heavens.
> Praise him for his acts of power;
> Praise him for his surpassing greatness.
> Praise him with the sounding of the trumpet,
> Praise him with the harp and lyre,
> Praise him with timbrel and dancing,
> Praise him with the strings and pipe,
> Praise him with the clash of cymbals,
> Praise him with resounding cymbals.
> Let everything that has breath praise the Jah.

Sabbath

The Sabbath is something often upheld by Rastafari. Although it is not practiced by every Rastafari, many keep this principle.[38] Bobo Ashanti is the most disciplined house when it comes to observing the Sabbath. They adopted it from the Bible's Old Testament. The Sabbath is on Saturdays, although it

---

38 www.tozion.org. (n.d.). *The Sabbath * Rastafari * ToZion.org *.* [online] Available at: https://www.tozion.org/Rasta-fari-Sabbath.html [Accessed 12 Aug. 2023]

begins on Friday at 6 p.m. and concludes on Saturday at 6 p.m. This is done so that people can prepare spiritually and because Bobo Ashanti use Ethiopian calendars, which indicate that the Sabbath is on Saturdays.[39] No work or financial transactions are permitted on the Sabbath. The first Sabbath, which is the first Sabbath of every month, is when all Bob Ashanti fast from midnight Saturday to 6 p.m. Saturday.

Comparatively, the Nyahbinghi and the Twelve Tribes are often less stringent in their observance of the Sabbath, and their practices may vary accordingly.

Ethiopia

Ethiopia, a land with a rich history and deep cultural significance, holds a unique place in the hearts of Rastafarians worldwide. Just as Mecca is to Muslims and Jerusalem is to Christians, Ethiopia stands as a spiritual and symbolic focal point for the Rastafarian movement. At the heart of this reverence lies its central figure of Emperor Haile Selassie, considered divine by Rastafarians, and the historical connections that have led to Ethiopia being often referred to as Zion.

The influence of Emperor Haile Selassie, born in Ethiopia, on Rastafarian beliefs cannot be overstated. He embodies the spiritual connection between Rastafarians and the land of Ethiopia, serving as a unifying figure around which their faith revolves. Rastafarians hold the belief that Haile Selassie's coronation fulfilled the prophecy of Marcus Garvey, a prediction that foresaw the crowning of a black king in Africa as a sign of imminent liberation. Garvey's words, "Look to Africa, when a black king shall be crowned, for the day of deliverance is at hand," became a cornerstone for the Rastafarian movement's aspirations for a holy and promised land of their own. In this context, Ethiopia emerges as a land of liberation and repatriation, echoing the yearnings of a marginalized community for identity and freedom.

The historical gesture of Emperor Haile Selassie providing land in Shashamene, Ethiopia, to black people who had supported him in his resistance against Mussolini's Italy underscores the tangible connection between Ethiopia and the Rastafarian community. In 1948, the emperor allocated 500 acres of land for this purpose, paving the way for the repatriation of Rastafarians

---

39 ibid

from the West, especially those who had played a role in fostering his cause. This move not only demonstrated a mutual bond but also enabled the Rastafarian movement to take a physical step towards its spiritual homeland.

The significance of Ethiopia within Rastafarian doctrine is further fortified by references from scriptural passages. Verses from the Bible, such as Genesis 2:13, Numbers 12:1, Jeremiah 13:23, Psalm 68:31 ("princes shall come out of Egypt, Ethiopia shall soon stretch forth her hands unto God"), and Psalm 87:4, are frequently cited to draw connections between Ethiopia and divine favor. These passages not only validate the spiritual resonance that Rastafarians feel toward Ethiopia but also offer a scriptural foundation for their beliefs.

One cannot ignore the historical context that intensifies the reverence Rastafarians hold for Ethiopia. Until 1935, Ethiopia remained unconquered by European powers, a remarkable feat in a colonial era marked by the subjugation of many African nations. This unblemished record of sovereignty, combined with its role as the birthplace of Emperor Haile Selassie, contributes to Ethiopia's exalted status as a beacon of hope and resilience for Rastafarians.

CHAPTER 6

Symbols

Symbols play a pivotal role in expressing the beliefs, values, and identity of different cultures and religious movements. Rastafarianism is no exception to this phenomenon. The Rastafarian movement employs a range of symbols to convey its spiritual, cultural, and social messages.

Hair Turban

Rastas put on turbans and can vary in style and color, and they may be worn in different ways by individuals within the movement, but it is Bobo Ashantis that are known for their tightly wrapped turbans on their dreadlocks. This essentially distinguishes them from the other mansions. However, not every Bobo Ashanti is eligible to wear a turban because the process begins when you become a convert and progresses through several phases. You may only wrap a turban if you agree and firmly adhere to the Bobo Ashanti order for a while, and it concludes with an official ceremony lead by a Bobo Ashanti priest. They put turbans on their heads to show that they are Bobo Ashanti members, as well as their worship and respect for Jah (God).

Long Robes

Rastafarian attire is the long robe, often referred to as a "gown" or "garment." These robes hold spiritual and symbolic significance within the Rastafarian belief system. Bobo Ashanti is identified for their colorful long robes. On the Sabbath, followers wear white long robes, both for men and women, and a turban.

Flags

The Rastafarian flags are another important symbol present in Rastafarian places of worship and camps, with two distinct types of flag used by the movement. These are shown in full colour on the back cover of this book (the final page of the electronic version).

The first flag features horizontal stripes in red, black, and green which can be traced back to the Universal Negro Improvement Association (UNIA). These colors hold specific significance: black symbolizes African heritage and identity, red signifies the sacrifices made in the struggle against colonialism, and green represents the fertile African land. The flag serves as a visible representation of the movement's dedication to African heritage, liberation, and unity.

The second flag is the Ethiopian flag that was used during Haile Selassie's reign, with three horizontal stripes in green, yellow, and red from top to bottom. Green is symbolic of Ethiopia's fertile landscapes, revered by Rastafarians as their spiritual homeland. Yellow represents the land's abundance. Red, on the other hand, symbolizes the bloodshed of those who fought for liberation, as well as the divine essence associated with Haile Selassie I.

Lion of Judah

To proclaim their identity, Rastas surround themselves with symbols and emblems depicting the lion. The choice of the lion as a Rastafarian symbol was doubtlessly influenced by the association of lions with Haile Selassie. According to Rastafarian mythology, Selassie descended from the tribe of

Judah, whose emblem was the lion, was born in the line of Solomon, who decorated the Solomonic temple with symbols of the lion, and was born under the astral sign of Leo (July 23). As part of his title, Selassie is identified as "the conquering lion of the tribe of Judah." Rastafarian tales tell of pet lions roaming freely through the imperial garden and the imperial palace. Furthermore, Selassie and his predecessors had a preoccupation with the lion: the lion's image is on their official seal, and lion statues "guard" the gates of the imperial palace.[40] Rastas seek to convey to others their sense of lion-ness, their self-confidence and self-assertiveness.[41]

Star of David

For the Rastafari, the Star of David is a significant protective emblem that connects Haile Selassie to the royal dynasties of King David and King Solomon. But its actual role in the faith varies depending on which branch of the movement one follows. For some, the Star of David is seen as a representation of the divinity, with each of its six points representing creativity, divine wisdom and power, justice, mercy, love, and eternity.[42]

Diamond-like Hand Gesture

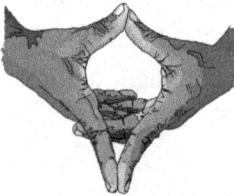

This emblem closely resembles the Rasta Star of David and was inspired from a popular hand gesture that Haile Selassie I used to portray himself. It's assumed that Haile performed this move to indicate that he is indeed a manifestation of the Divine, also known as the Seal of Solomon or the Diamond Hand Gesture. Many Rastafarians today make this motion when they are praying.[43]

In essence, symbols are integral to the Rastafarian movement's expression of identity, spirituality, and cultural values. From the distinctive turbans of the Bobo Ashanti to the Lion of Judah and the Star of David, each symbol carries layers of meaning that reflect the movement's history, beliefs, and aspirations. Through these symbols, Rastafarians communicate their devotion to their faith, their African heritage, and their vision of unity and liberation.

40 Edmonds, op.cit.
41 ibid
42 Club, A.N.Z.R. (2023). *Why do Rastas use the Star of David?* [online] www.newzealandrabbitclub.net. Available at: https://www.newzealandrabbitclub.net/why-do-rastas-use-the-star-of-david/
43 Symbol Sage. (2021). *List of Rastafarian Symbols and Their Meaning.* [online] Available at: https://symbolsage.com/rastafarian-symbols-list-meaning/

CHAPTER 7

Rituals & Practices

Rituals and practices not only shape the Rastafarian identity but also reflect a profound commitment to a holistic and spiritually meaningful existence.

Marijuana

Contrary to popular misconceptions, the use of marijuana, or ganja as referred to by Rastafarians, is not merely a recreational indulgence but holds profound religious significance within the faith. The act of smoking marijuana is not about seeking a state of getting high but rather a way to commune with the divine. The Bobo Ashanti sect, for instance, believes that the consumption of marijuana is permissible only when it is conducted as an act of worship. This underscores the spiritual intent behind its use, emphasizing that it is not about getting high, but about connecting with the divine and attaining a higher state of consciousness.

The sacred nature of marijuana is intertwined with biblical references. Passages such as "The herb is the healing of the nations" (Revelation 22:2) and "eat every herb of the land" (Exodus 10:12) highlight the role of natural substances in spiritual healing and sustenance. This connection between ancient scriptures and the Rastafarian practice of using marijuana in rituals reinforces the faith's rootedness in ancient wisdom.

"Ital" livity

The concept of "Ital" living embodies the Rastafarian ideal of living in harmony with nature and rejecting the artificiality of modern society. This commitment to naturalness extends to various aspects of life, including diet and material consumption. By adhering to a vegetarian diet and consuming organic, unprocessed foods.[44] Thus, Rastas, are strictly vegetarian and rarely eat meat. It's also based on the Holy scriptures such as Gen 1:29: "And God said, Behold, I have given you every herb bearing seed, which is upon the face of all the earth, and every tree, in the which is the fruit of a tree yielding seed; to you it shall be for meat." (KJV)

The rejection of synthetic materials and chemically treated foods underlines the Rastafarian rejection of the consumer-driven, materialistic culture often

44 Edmonds, E. B. (2002). *Rastafari: From Outcasts to Culture Bearers.* New York, Oxford University Press

associated with Babylon. By embracing Ital living, Rastafarians express their longing for a simpler, more connected way of life, reflecting their desire to return to their African roots and restore their bond with nature.

In today's world a vegan diet has been adopted by many people due to its health benefits.

Holy days

Rastafarianism reveres and commemorates a range of holy days that hold deep spiritual and cultural significance. These occasions provide opportunities for communal worship, reflection, and a reaffirmation of the faith's core principles.

Groundation Day, 21 April

This day marks the visit of Haile Selassie I to Jamaica in 1966. Rastafarians celebrate through rituals, ceremonies, and prayers, underscoring the spiritual and cultural connections between Ethiopia and the Rastafarian movement. These celebrations often involve music, drumming, chanting, and the reading of sacred texts.

Coronation, 2 November

This is one of the most sacred days for Rastafarians across the world. It commemorates the 1930 coronation of Haile Selassie as emperor of Ethiopia, which is a pivotal event. He assumed the names Haile Selassie and "Might of the Trinity," as well as the titles "King of Kings, Lord of Lords, and Conquering Lion of the Tribe of Judah."

Marcus Garvey's Birthday, 17 August

As a prophet and a figure integral to Rastafarian beliefs, Marcus Garvey is honored on this day. The celebration serves as a reminder of the importance of unity among Africans. Garvey had anticipated the appearance of Haile Selassie as a king.

Emperor Selassie's birthday – celebrated on 23 July

On this day, Rastafarians celebrate the life and teachings of Emperor Haile Selassie I. It is a time of reflection on his legacy and its significance within the faith.

Ethiopian New Year

11 September is a holiday to commemorate Ethiopian history. The global history of Rastafari is intertwined with Ethiopian history. It is a place of pilgrimage and the promised land for Rastafari followers.

Ethiopian Christmas, 7 January

Rastafarians celebrate Christmas on 7 January, following the Ethiopian Orthodox calendar. This date marks the birth of Jesus Christ. Rastafarians often refer to Jesus as "Jah" and view him as a significant figure in their faith.

These holy days play a crucial role in reinforcing the Rastafari identity, promoting a sense of community, and fostering a deeper spiritual connection among followers. The celebrations often involve prayer, meditation, feasting, music (especially reggae), drumming, and chanting of Rastafarian hymns. Through these observances, Rastafarians express their devotion to Haile Selassie, their African heritage, and their commitment to social justice and equality.

CHAPTER 8

Religious and Philosophical Literature

The Rastafari movement reveres a collection of religious writings that extend beyond the confines of the conventional Bible. Central to this expanded literary canon are texts such as *The Holy Piby*, the *Kebra Negast*, *The Promised Key*, *My Life and Ethiopia's Progress*, and *The Royal Parchment Scroll of Black Supremacy*. Each of these texts plays a crucial role in shaping Rastafari beliefs, connecting followers to their African heritage, and asserting a unique theological perspective.

The Holy Piby: The Black Man's Bible

The Holy Piby, also known as the "Black Man's Bible," is a foundational text in Rastafari literature published in 1924. It was compiled by Robert Athlyi Rogers and contains a mixture of Afrocentric religious teachings and interpretations of the Bible. The book glorifies and portrays Ethiopia as the land of the chosen people. Although it was not produced expressly for Rastafari, it is considered a foundation document of Rastafarian ideology because it influenced Rastafari founders among other literatures.

The Holy Piby is divided into three main sections;

The First Book of Athlyi Called Athlyi: This section lays out the beliefs and teachings of the *Holy Piby*, including the creation of the African race and the divine mission of black people. It has two chapters.

The Second Book of Athlyi Called Second Athlyi: This section continues to expound upon the religious and philosophical principles of the *Holy Piby*, emphasizing the importance of black unity and self-empowerment.

The Third Book of Athlyi Called Third Athlyi: This section provides further teachings and guidance for followers of the *Holy Piby*, discussing topics such as prophecy, rituals, and the destiny of the African race.

Kebra Negast

The *Kebra Negast*, also referred to as "The Glory of Kings," was written in the 14th century. It is a sacred scripture that covers Ethiopian Orthodox Christianity, and it is regarded as a reliable historical work.

It connects the origins of Ethiopia's Solomonic dynasty to the Queen of Sheba (also known as Makeda in Ethiopia) and King Solomon in Jerusalem. It was thought to be divinely inspired and hence properly legitimized Haile Selassie dynasty's tie to the Solomonic dynasty. However, Ethiopian Christians only regard it as a historical epic of Ethiopian royalty. To Rastafarians, *Kebra Negast* is holy and a manifestation of Emperor Haile Selassie, who is a reincarnation of God.

The book opens with an interpretation and explanation of the Three Hundred and Eighteen Orthodox Fathers concerning the children of Adam, and the statement that the Trinity lived in Zion, the Tabernacle of the Law of God, which God made in the fortress of His holiness before He made anything else. The Trinity agreed to make man in God's image, and the Son agreed to put on the flesh of Adam; man was made to take the place of Satan and to praise God. In due course Christ, the second Adam, was born of the flesh of Mary the Virgin, the Second Zion. (Chapter 1)[45]

Kebra Negast is one of the books that devotees of the Rastafari religion adopt because of the similarities between historical figures and biblical characters that give it a sacred status.

The Promised Key

Rastafari movement pioneer Leonard P. Howell penned *The Promised Key* in 1935 in Jamaica. As the first Rasta, he is regarded as such. In addition to serving as a religious teaching tool, this book also serves as a rallying cry for Rastafarians and other black people. At the time it was written, there was a global suppression of black people's freedom. At the time, Haile Selassie was hailed as the messiah and Ethiopia as the Promised Land by Howell through the Promised Key, who lived in Jamaica, then a British colony. The Bobo Ashanti have continued to honor and adore Haile Selassie ever since *The Promised Key* revealed him to be divine.

My Life and Ethiopia's Progress

Emperor Haile Selassie's autobiography, *My Life and Ethiopia's Progress*, occupies a significant place in the Rastafari literary canon. Providing insights into Haile Selassie's life journey, the text contributes to the perception of him as a key figure within the Rastafari belief system. His life story, intertwined with

---

45 Sacred-texts.com. (n.d.). The Kebra Nagast: Introduction: V. Summary of the Contents of the Kĕbra Nagast. [online] Available at: https://sacred-texts.com/afr/kn/kn008.htm.

Ethiopia's progress, is regarded as a testament to the transformation of man into the divine, reinforcing his spiritual importance within Rastafarianism.

The Royal Parchment Scroll of Black Supremacy

Authored by Rastafarian elder Fitz Balintine Pettersburg in the 1920s, *The Royal Parchment Scroll of Black Supremacy* emphasizes themes of racial pride and Africa's pivotal role in shaping the world's history. This text aligns with the broader Rastafari ethos of reclaiming African identity and dismantling the colonial narratives that suppressed it. The scroll's teachings resonate deeply with Rastafarians, fostering a sense of pride rooted in their heritage.

Religious literature holds immense importance within Rastafarianism for several reasons: In shaping Rastafarian beliefs, texts such as *The Holy Piby, Kebra Negast, The Promised Key, My Life and Ethiopia's Progress* and *The Royal Parchment Scroll of Black Supremacy* serve as foundational documents that shape and define Rastafarian beliefs and practices. They provide a theological framework and guidance for followers.

Connection to African heritage: Rastafarianism places a strong emphasis on reconnecting with African roots and heritage. Many of these texts, especially *The Holy Piby* and *The Royal Parchment Scroll of Black Supremacy* celebrate African culture, history, and identity. They assert that Africa is the cradle of humanity and that black people are the chosen people of God.

Legitimizing Haile Selassie's divinity: Kebra Negast plays a crucial role in legitimizing the divine status of Emperor Haile Selassie within Rastafarianism. It connects him to biblical figures, reinforcing the belief that he is a reincarnation of God. This association is central to Rastafarian theology.

Providing historical and religious context: Kebra Negast and *My Life and Ethiopia's Progress* offer historical and biographical insights into Ethiopia, its monarchy, and Haile Selassie. These texts help Rastafarians contextualize their beliefs within the broader historical and religious narrative.

Unity and Empowerment: The Holy Piby and *The Promised Key* emphasize the importance of black unity and self-empowerment. They inspire Rastafarians to unite as a community and take pride in their identity as black people.

Resistance to colonial narratives: The Royal Parchment Scroll of Black Supremacy challenges colonial narratives that denigrated African culture and history. It encourages Rastafarians to reject the oppressive ideologies of colonialism and embrace their African heritage with pride.

Spiritual guidance: Many of these texts, including *The Holy Piby* and *The Promised Key,* offer spiritual guidance, rituals, and teachings that help Rastafarians navigate their faith and spiritual journey. They provide a roadmap for living according to Rastafarian principles.

Distinctive theological perspective: Collectively, these texts offer a distinctive theological perspective that distinguishes Rastafarianism from mainstream Christianity. They reinterpret traditional religious concepts, such as the role of Ethiopia and the divinity of Haile Selassie, according to Rastafarian beliefs.

In summary, these religious texts are essential to Rastafarianism because they provide a spiritual foundation, connect followers to their African heritage, legitimize the divine status of Haile Selassie, promote unity and empowerment, challenge colonial narratives, and offer a unique theological perspective. They are not just literary works but sacred scriptures that guide and inspire Rastafarians in their beliefs and practices.

CHAPTER 9

Conclusion

This chapter concludes with an analysis on inquiry and criticisms, yet leaves its themes open-ended, inviting the reader to continue the exploration in their own lives, interactions, and perspectives.

Patriarchy and the Oppression of Women in Rastafarianism

Rastafarianism has been known for its revolutionary ideals and resistance against social injustices. However, while the movement has often focused on uplifting the marginalized and oppressed, it is essential to critically examine the role of women within Rastafarianism. Despite their significant presence and contributions, women's experiences and perspectives have been marginalized, and the movement's association with patriarchy and the oppression of women demands a careful analysis and not over romanization of the movement.

From the early days of Rastafarianism, women and children have been integral to the movement's growth and development. However, scholarly research into the substantial role women have played remains limited, resulting in an inadequate representation of their contributions. This imbalance in historical documentation has led to an incomplete understanding of Rastafarianism and its evolution. Within the movement, women are often referred to as "queens," and "empresses,". These titles may initially seem empowering, elevating women beyond the confines of Western constructs. Yet, a closer examination reveals that these labels can also reinforce stereotypes and predefined gender roles. Similar to many religious systems, Rastafarianism relies heavily on biblical texts, which inadvertently perpetuate patriarchal norms and contribute to the oppression of women.

Certain Rastafarian mansions, such as the Bobo Ashanti, adhere to traditional practices that discriminate against women. For example, women are barred from entering the tabernacle during menstruation and for a considerable period afterward. Such practices reinforce the perception of women as impure during menstruation, relegating them to a state of inferiority. Additionally, notions of submission and obedience further underscore the patriarchal framework within the Bobo Ashanti community. Men's authority as heads of households is maintained, thereby limiting women's autonomy and potential.

Rastafarianism's gender dynamics are deeply influenced by biblical interpretations and cultural norms that have evolved over time in Jamaica and globally. This male-dominated structure is reinforced by scriptural and male Rastafarian teachings, which place women in subservient roles. While women have a presence within the movement, by adhering to these teachings coupled with culture results in a scenario where Rastafarian women may experience oppression from multiple fronts, sstemming from their blackness, religious beliefs, gender, and economic contexts. The patriarchal framework of Rastafarianism intersects with societal norms, limiting women's agency and perpetuating their marginalization. In this context, the movement's resistance to systemic oppression can paradoxically reinforce the subjugation of its own women.

Rastafarianism's rich history of resistance and liberation is marked by the struggle against various forms of oppression. However, it is crucial to recognize that the movement itself is not immune to perpetuating patriarchy and the oppression of women.

Nevertheless, over the years, there have been dialogues and efforts within the Rastafari community to address gender disparities and promote gender equality like in 12 tries of Israel mansion. Also, some Rastafarian women have been outspoken about challenging traditional gender roles and advocating for women's rights within the movement. This includes promoting women's leadership, challenging discriminatory practices, and fostering a more inclusive and equitable Rastafari culture.

Rastafarianism in the Context of Ethiopia: Promised Land Aspirations

Rastafarianism, has long been characterized by its fervent belief that Africa is its ancestral homeland, with Ethiopia standing as the coveted Promised Land. A core tenet of Rastafarian belief revolves around the idea that repatriation to Africa, particularly to Ethiopia is their final journey. But how easy is it to fulfill spiritual yearning with real-world challenges.? Eric Macleod's work *Visions of Zion: Ethiopians and Rastafari in the Search for the Promised Land* explores these dynamics and sheds light on the intricate relationship between Rastafarian migrants and the Ethiopian society in which they seek to integrate.

Rastafarian reverence for Ethiopia is rooted in their conviction that it is the spiritual and geographical center of their faith. This sentiment is manifested in the pilgrimage to the town of Shashamane in southern Ethiopia, where Rastafarians from across the globe converge in a testament to their unwavering devotion. The movement gained added significance when Emperor Haile Selassie, revered as a messianic figure by Rastafarians, donated 500 acres of land to the movement in Jamaica. This gesture not only reinforced the deep spiritual connection between Rastafarians and Ethiopia but also ignited a complex set of interactions between Rastafarian migrants and the Ethiopian population.

Macleod's analysis highlights the challenges that underlie the Rastafarian endeavor to repatriate to Ethiopia. A central predicament lies in the differing perceptions between Rastafarian migrants and the local Ethiopian populace. While Rastafarians arrive with the expectation of being embraced as long-lost African brethren, the Ethiopian reality paints a more nuanced picture. The historical and cultural context shapes Ethiopians' view of migrating Rastafarians as outsiders. This dichotomy in perception forms a barrier to seamless integration and mutual understanding.

It is only in recent times that the Ethiopian government has begun to issue national residence cards to Rastafarians who have resided in the country for over a decade. This step signifies a degree of recognition and legal acknowledgment, but it also underscores the protracted struggles Rastafarians faced for official documentation since their first influx in the 1950s. The absence of proper permits or identification cards forced many Rastafarians to navigate their status as "illegal residents," resorting to unconventional means to facilitate travel beyond Ethiopian borders.

Despite efforts towards integration, the journey towards realizing the Rastafarian dream of repatriation remains fraught with challenges. Interactions with the local population have led to both inter-marriages and clashes with neighbors. The veneration of Haile Selassie, a divine figure in Rastafarianism, contrasts sharply with the opinions of some Ethiopians who view him as a colonial dictator, particularly among the Oromo people. The geographical context compounds tensions, as the land allocated by Selassie to Rastafarians is situated within regions inhabited by the Oromo, a community that claims historical oppression under the Amhara, Selassie's dominant ethnic group.

Another source of discord revolves around the spiritual use of marijuana within the Rastafarian faith. While it holds profound significance as a sacrament, neighbors perceive it as a dangerous drug with potentially harmful effects on young people. This divide in understanding further accentuates the cultural chasm between Rastafarians and their Ethiopian counterparts.

While Ethiopia remains the spiritual beacon for Rastafarians worldwide, the realization of their repatriation dreams proves far from straightforward. The disparities in perception, historical context, and cultural clashes serve as reminders that the journey towards the Promised Land is a protracted and evolving endeavor.

Why Dar es Salaam Over Ethiopia: A Haven for Revolutionaries

The choice of exile destination for Pan-Africanist and African Marxist intellectuals during the tumultuous years of the 1960s to the 1980s raises a compelling question: Why did they prefer Dar es Salaam in Tanzania over Ethiopia, a nation steeped in history and culture of, and the birthplace of the Organization of African Unity (OAU) established on 25 May 1963?

Tanzania was a haven for political exiles like Walter Rodney, the December Twelve Movement from Kenya, the Black Panther Party, Samora Machel and national liberation movements in Africa such as the Frelimo and ANC. There are several reasons why Tanzania was the preferred destination for most revolutionaries through the 1960s-80s, we can decipher from articles such as *The Dar es Salaam years* by Leo Zeilig, Walter Rodney's *Dar es Salaam Years, 1966–1974* by Immanuel R Harisch and *The Mecca of African Liberation: Walter Rodney in Tanzania* by Chinedu Chukwudinma.

Tanzania, under the leadership of President Julius Nyerere, was known for its strong commitment to Pan-Africanism and solidarity with liberation movements across the African continent. Nyerere's government actively supported various African liberation struggles and welcomed political exiles from other African countries who were fighting against colonialism, apartheid, or oppressive regimes. This stance made Tanzania an attractive destination for political activists and revolutionaries. Dar es Salaam, then the capital city of Tanzania, emerged as a hub for intellectual and cultural exchange during this era. It beckoned scholars, writers, and activists from diverse corners of Africa and the world. The city's vibrancy, coupled with its openness to ideas and innovation, provided an ideal environment for intellectual ferment. The free exchange of ideas and experiences nurtured the intellectual growth of those who sought refuge in Dar es Salaam.

Further, President Nyerere and his government were not merely sympathetic to the causes of liberation movements; they actively championed them. Tanzania provided not only sanctuary but also practical assistance, including training facilities, material aid, and diplomatic support, to numerous liberation movements. Walter Rodney, a prominent Marxist historian and activist, found his views aligning with the socialist policies of Nyerere's government, making Tanzania a natural choice for him and others who shared similar ideological leanings.

Also, Tanzania's diplomatic ties with various countries worldwide, including the Soviet Union and other Eastern Bloc nations, played a pivotal role in attracting political exiles. These diplomatic relations allowed Tanzania to establish connections with political movements and governments that mirrored its socialist and anti-imperialist stance. Consequently, it became relatively easy for revolutionary figures to relocate to Tanzania, where they could find both a safe haven and ideological alignment.

In contrast, Ethiopia, despite its rich historical significance and being the birthplace of the OAU, did not emerge as the preferred destination for many revolutionaries under Haile Sellasie Monarch. One crucial factor could be Ethiopia's alignment, or lack thereof, with the objectives of specific liberation movements. Revolutionary intellectuals and activists often sought refuge in countries whose governments shared their ideological and political goals. Ethiopia's monarchy while considered holy by Rastas, for instance, maintained a close relationship with British imperialism, which could have deterred revolutionaries who opposed colonial powers.

Walter Rodney's Perception of the Rastafari Movement

Walter Rodney, born in 1942, was a distinguished Guyanese historian, political activist, and scholar whose profound contributions to African history and his unwavering advocacy for social justice continues to resonate today. He is celebrated for his groundbreaking work, *How Europe Underdeveloped Africa*, his doctoral thesis on the Upper Guinea Coast, and his engagement with marginalized communities, particularly the Rastafarians in Jamaica. Rodney's life and work are a testament to his dedication to fighting against oppression, which was exemplified by the tumultuous events of the 1968 Rodney Riots in Kingston, Jamaica and his impact on the global south.

On 15 October 1968, the Jamaican government prevented Walter Rodney from returning to the island. Rodney, a lecturer at the University of the West Indies (UWI) Mona campus, had been abroad attending a Black Power conference in Canada. He had graduated from UWI in 1963. He returned to UWI in early 1968 after completing graduate studies in England and briefly working in Tanzania.[46]

Rodney's second stint in Jamaica lasted only nine months but was marked by significant turmoil both within and outside the university. The decision to ban him led to major disturbances, including a riot in the capital city of Kingston. The U.S. government, represented by its embassy in Kingston, closely monitored what became known as the "Rodney affair" and the significant impact it had on highlighting the Black Power movement.[47]

Rodney was more than just a scholar; he was a passionate advocate for social change. His radical political views and tireless efforts to champion the rights of marginalized groups, including Rastafarians, made him a revolutionary intellectual who transcended the boundaries of academia. He engaged in dialogue with Rastafarians, seeing their struggle for social justice as part of a broader movement for Black liberation and empowerment. In his 1969 book, *Groundings with My Brothers,* Rodney explored the social and political perspectives of Rastafarians, expressing deep sympathy for their cause. He recognized the Rastafari movement as a vital component of the broader struggle for black liberation. He saw in the Rastafarians a group of individuals who were passionately dedicated to dismantling the oppressive structures of white imperialism. The Rastafarians, often marginalized and misunderstood by mainstream society, were, in Rodney's eyes, a force to be reckoned with in the battle for emancipation.

As Horace Campbell puts it, Rodney believed that the Rastafarians were not merely passive observers of the struggle for liberation; they actively participated in efforts to free and mobilize black minds. Their commitment to this cause was evident in their unwavering dedication to their beliefs and principles. The Rastafarians sought to break the myths perpetuated by white imperialism and replace them with a profound sense of self-awareness and cultural identity.[48]

46 www.marxists.org. (2006). *The Targeting of Walter Rodney* | Solidarity. [online] Available at: https://www.marxists.org/history/etol/newspape/atc/136.html
47 ibid
48 Campbell, H. (1987). *Rasta and Resistance*. New Jersey, Africa World Press, Inc.

Walter Rodney's legacy extends far beyond his academic resume and the turmoil of the Rodney Riots. As a revolutionary intellectual he challenged oppressive systems and advocated for social justice, leaving an indelible mark on the global south. Remarkably, his association with Rastafarianism, often misunderstood and marginalized, speaks to the depth of his commitment to uplifting the voices of the marginalized. The Rastafarians were not only a religious or cultural movement; they were a force of resistance and empowerment. Their rejection of societal norms and their commitment to living their African heritage served as a powerful example for others seeking to break free from the shackles of white imperialism. Rodney recognized that the Rastafarians were at the forefront of a broader awakening, pushing for a more inclusive and equitable world where the dignity and humanity of black people were acknowledged and celebrated.

After his assassination in 1980, Rodney's influence on Rastafarianism endures, with reggae artists like Linton Kwesi Johnson, Louie Lepkie, and Ky-Mani Marley among others paying tribute to his memory with popular reggae songs.

Bob Marley and the Commercialization of Rastafarianism

The evolution of Rastafarianism, along with its notable figureheads, has undergone significant transformation over the years. Some critics argue that Rastafarianism, once a radical and revolutionary movement, has now become overly commercialized, losing its initial vigor and adopting new values and lifestyles.

Robert Nesta Marley, affectionately known as Bob Marley, was not just a musician; he was a cultural icon, a voice for change, and a symbol of hope for many. Born 6 February 1945 in the vibrant and culturally rich island of Jamaica, Marley would go on to leave an indelible mark on the world through his music, beliefs, and unwavering dedication to the causes he held dear.

At the heart of Bob Marley's legacy lies his profound connection to Jamaican music and culture. His music transcended borders, capturing the hearts and minds of people from all corners of the globe. With his soulful reggae rhythms and meaningful lyrics, Marley's music became a powerful tool for expressing the struggles, dreams, and aspirations of not only Jamaicans but also marginalized communities worldwide.

He was also a fearless advocate for democratic social reforms, unafraid to use his platform to address the pressing issues of his time. His outspoken support for change often courted controversy, but it also galvanized countless individuals to join the fight for justice and equality and this characterized the essence of Rastafarianism. However, it is essential to examine how the conscious commodification of his music gradually undermined its aesthetic and ideological essence as it is today.

The erosion of the ideological substance of Rastafarianism, exemplified by Bob Marley's journey, can be traced through his association with major record companies from the 1970s to the 1990s.[49] As these artists encountered Western economic hegemony, they often found themselves making creative compromises, thus setting a precedent for the commercialization of reggae within the music industry that ultimately influenced Rastafarianism.

One striking example of the commercialization of Bob Marley and Rastafarianism is the widespread use of his image and likeness for commercial purposes. While Bob Marley once symbolized resistance and revolution through reggae music, his image has been commodified and exploited for profit. This commodification takes various forms, such as the use of his face on merchandise like t-shirts, posters, hats, and clothing items. These products are often sold as fashion statements, devoid of any connection to the political beliefs and ideals Marley espoused during his lifetime. In addition to merchandise, Bob Marley's image has been incorporated into various forms of art and popular culture, including music, movies, and street art. Some use his image to make statements about rebellion and counterculture, while others do so purely for aesthetic or shock value.

The commercialization of Bob Marley's image has sparked intense debate and criticism within both Rastafarian and global communities. Some argue that this commodification dilutes and trivializes his revolutionary legacy, reducing him to a mere fashion icon or marketing tool. Others view it as a form of cultural appropriation or exploitation, as it often divorces his image from its original meaning.

While, proponents of this commercial use argue that it helps keep Bob Marley's memory and ideas alive, even if done in a commercial manner. As it also introduces his music and Rastafarianism to new audiences who may not have otherwise encountered them.

---

49 Alleyne, M. (1998). Babylon Makes the Rules: The Politics of Reggae Crossover. *Social and Economic Studies*, 47(1), 65–77. https://www.jstor.org/stable/27866166

Nevertheless, the commercialization of Bob Marley and Rastafarianism has had a profound effect on the movement. Rastafarianism is now associated with tourist attractions and a call for peace and love, marking a stark departure from its radical roots. The commercialization has transformed it from a revolutionary ideology into a marketable brand, which, while promoting elements of unity and spirituality, has diluted its original message of resistance against oppressive systems.

Haile Selassie: A Controversial Figure

Rastafarianism, as a religious and cultural movement, has at its core a deep reverence for Emperor Haile Selassie I of Ethiopia. Selassie is considered by many Rastafarians to be a divine figure, the embodiment of God, and the promised messiah who will lead black people to redemption. However, the perception of Haile Selassie is far from unanimous among Pan Africanists and historians.

Emperor Haile Selassie's reputation as a symbol of African resistance against colonialism is rooted in his leadership during the First Italo-Ethiopian War (1895-1896) and the Second Italo-Ethiopian War (1935-1936). His unwavering determination to defend Ethiopia's sovereignty in the face of Italian aggression earned him admiration from Rastafarians and many Africans. Also, Selassie's decision to provide headquarters for the first-ever home for the Organization of African Unity (O.A.U) further solidified his status as a pan-Africanist leader.

Nevertheless, in contrast to the romanticized and revered image of Haile Selassie, some scholars, such as Woldemariam (2019), calls for a more critical examination of his legacy. According to Woldemariam, the portrayal of Selassie as a benevolent ruler and champion of black people is a distortion of history. He argues that there are no facts supporting Selassie as a true pan-Africanist and revolutionary leader.

Woldemariam's perspective raises important questions about Selassie's actions during key historical events. For instance, Selassie's flight from Mussolini's troops in 1935 during the Italian invasion of Ethiopia led to criticism from prominent figures like Marcus Garvey. Garvey condemned Selassie as a "great coward" for fleeing in the face of danger, which challenges the perception of him as an unwavering leader of African resistance. Furthermore, it is essential to acknowledge that Ethiopia continued the practice of slavery until 1942, a fact that further complicates Selassie's legacy.[50] Garvey, a significant influence (prophet) in Rastafarianism, criticized Selassie's involvement in this practice and questioned his commitment to the liberation of Black people.

Another aspect of Haile Selassie's legacy is his international standing as a statesman. While he is often remembered for his powerful speeches on the global stage, it is essential to recognize that his prominence was largely due to his role as a loyal client of the West. Like other client leaders such as the Shah of Iran and Mobutu of Zaire, Selassie maintained power through repression and the suppression of dissent.[51]

Further, Haile Selassie's rule in Ethiopia was characterized by its autocratic nature. He resisted calls for political reforms and democratization, leading to his eventual overthrow by Mengistu revolutionary movement in 1974. The onset of the takeover can be traced back to the Selassie regime's inability to implement economic and political changes. This, coupled with issues such as inflation, corruption, and famine in the northeastern regions due to drought, led to military unrest that rapidly disseminated throughout the civilian populace, sparking a nationwide revolution. Selassie's rule faced widespread opposition due to a variety of complaints, including increased fuel costs, alterations to the education system, inadequate teacher salaries, unfavorable working conditions overall, and the demand for land reform against the monarchy.[52]

This aspect of his rule challenges the notion of Selassie as a benevolent and visionary leader in Ethiopia. The contrasting views of Selassie's legacy high-light's the dynamic nature of Rastafarianism and the need for a nuanced understanding of its central figure. Ultimately, the debate surrounding Haile Selassie's legacy serves as a reminder of the importance of critically examining historical figures and the narratives that surround them, always analyzing the other side of the story that is never told.

---

50 Africa at LSE. (2019). *The romantic rewriting of Haile Selassie's legacy must stop.* [online] Available at: https://blogs.lse.ac.uk/africaatlse/2019/02/04/the-romantic-rewriting-of-haile-selassies-legacy-must-stop/

51 ibid

52 adst.org. (2016). Anatomy of an Overthrow: How an African Leader was Toppled – *Association for Diplomatic Studies & Training.* [online] Available at: https://adst.org/2016/10/anatomy-overthrow-revered-African-leader-toppled [Accessed 27 Sept. 2023]

Rastafarianism, Israel, Palestine: Exploring Beliefs and Oppression

Rastafarianism has always gained attention for its unique blend of beliefs root-ed in Judaism, Christianity, and African traditions. One of the key aspects of Rastafarianism is its reliance on the Old Testament of the Bible, which leads to a deep reverence for Israel. However, this alignment with Israel's historical significance stands in stark contrast to the stance taken by many other social justice movements, particularly in relation to the Israel-Palestine conflict.

Rastafarianism's theological foundation draws parallels with Judaism and Christianity, with a strong emphasis on the Old Testament narratives. This connection has led Rastafarians to view Israel as a sacred land, reflecting the historical and spiritual journey of their own beliefs. While Rastafarianism is inherently spiritual and transcendent, it tends to focus on the metaphysical realm rather than engaging with political conflicts on the material reality. This is where Rastafarianism diverges from various left-leaning social movements that advocate for justice, including Palestine.

In contemporary discourse, left-leaning social movements, progressive scholars, and political parties often scrutinize the actions of Israel in the con-text of the oppression faced by the Palestinian people. Social movements con-demn Israel as an imperialist and colonial force in the Middle East, drawing attention to the complexities of the Israel-Palestine conflict and advocating for the rights and self-determination of Palestinians. However, Rastafarianism tends to takes an unusual approach by not aligning itself with either side of the conflict and focusing primarily on its spiritual aspects, that are tied to Israel.

Take for instance, Bob Marley's son, Ziggy Marley in 2015, when he was awarded the Jewish National Fund's Shalom Peace Award and expressed his deep connection to Israel through his upbringing. He mentioned his family's strong belief in the history of Israel and the personal and spiritual connec-tion they feel towards the land and its people.[53] This shows how Rastafarian-ism's spiritual beliefs can become abstract and oblivious to the struggles of the people.

Rastafarianism's emphasis on "peace and love" is a common theme in reggae music and the movement itself. However, the concepts of peace and love can

53 Musodza, M. (2015). *The Ties That Bind: Reggae, Rastafari, Judaism and Israel.* [online] blogs.timesofisrael.com.
   Available at: https://blogs.timesofisrael.com/the-ties-that-bind-reggae-rastafari-judaism-and-israel/

sometimes appear apolitical in the face of struggles for national self-determi-nation. While Rastafarianism promotes these principles, it is often criticized for not taking a more active stance against oppressive systems and for not aligning with social justice causes such as the Western Sahrawi people's quest for self-determination or the struggles of the Kurdish people.

Rastafarianism's lack of political alignment in cases of oppression and social injustice, such as the Israel-Palestine conflict, highlights the nuanced nature of this movement. Its primary focus remains on its spiritual aspects rather than tak-ing explicit positions on geopolitical conflicts, which many find problematic.

Because religion and capitalism, while two distinct realms of humanity, have often intersected and intertwined, particularly in the context of the Western world that Rastas call Babylon. This relationship has led to the sanitization of oppression and inequalities, offering promises of a better world after worldly suffering. However, the perpetuation of inequality and exploitation reveals the inadequacy of this partnership in addressing systemic issues. The Rastafarian movement, while condemning the Babylon system, seemingly falls short in comprehending the systemic issues that are fundamentally human-made rather than solely attributed to individual failings.

In today's world, the convergence of religion and capitalism is evident through the lens of neoliberal, free-market politics. Neoliberalism emphasizes mini-mal government intervention in economic affairs, promoting individualism, competition, and deregulation. This alignment is rooted in the idea that mate-rial prosperity and spiritual salvation are achievable hand-in-hand. Capitalism promises a path to prosperity through economic growth and accumulation of wealth, while religion offers spiritual salvation and hope for a better life after death. This synthesis has led to the belief that economic success and spiritual righteousness are interconnected, reinforcing the notion that one's achieve-ments are indicative of moral position.

The combination of religion and capitalism can also serve to sanitize oppres-sion and inequality. By promising rewards in the afterlife for enduring suf-fering in the present world, this alliance can quell resistance against social injustices. The idea that inequality is not a systemic issue but rather a tempo-rary phase to be rectified in the afterlife can foster complacency among those experiencing hardship, a phenomenon with the Rastafari. This is particularly evident in cases where economic disparities are explained away as part of a divine plan or a test of faith. Consequently, addressing systemic inequality can take a backseat, as the focus shifts towards personal piety and the pursuit of economic success.

The entwined narratives of religion and capitalism can lead to the creation of illusory happiness. By promising spiritual rewards and material prosperity, this partnership can veil the harsh realities of exploitation and inequality. The idea that suffering will be redemptive in the afterlife or that hard work will inevitably lead to prosperity can obscure the injustices that persist in the present. This result in a society that is willing to accept cruelty and exploitation, as long as the promise of eventual salvation or success remains intact.

The synthesis of religion and capitalism in the Western context raises profound questions about the nature of societal structures, morality, and justice. How can a system that perpetuates inequality and exploitation be reconciled with the principles of compassion and fairness that many religions uphold including Rastafarianism? What is the role of Rastafarianism in holding capitalism accountable for its impact on vulnerable communities? And how can movements like Rastafarianism evolve to address not only the surface-level symptoms but also the systemic roots of oppression?

While Rastafarianism's critique of the Babylon system is valid, their vision of an alternative society might not adequately address the complexities of systemic exploitation. There is the need for a deeper understanding of systemic issues. As societies continue to grapple with these intricate intersections, it becomes imperative to confront the illusory happiness perpetuated by this synthesis and to seek a more equitable and just path forward, one that acknowledges the systemic nature of inequality and exploitation, and actively works to dismantle them.

Glossary

Assembly of Elders: Refers to a group or council of older, respected individuals who play a significant role in decision-making within the Rastafari community.

Babylon: In the context of Rastafari it's a symbolic concept representing the forces of colonization, imperialism, racism, and social injustice. The term "Babylon" originates from the Biblical story of the Tower of Babel, which is used metaphorically to describe a society that opposes the values of Rastafarianism.

Bob Marley: Popular reggae artist from Jamaica. Through his music Rastafari spread to the world.

Black Uhuru: Reggae band from Jamaica formed in 1972. Through its music Rastafari spread all over the world.

Colonisation: The process by which one country or group of people establish control over another territory, often with the aim of exploiting its resources, establishing settlements, and exerting political, economic, and cultural influence.

Declaration: The Universal Declaration of Human Rights is an international document adopted by the United Nations General Assembly that enshrines the rights and freedoms of all human beings.

Emperor: An emperor is a monarch who holds the highest rank in a hierarchical structure of nobility and sovereignty.

Emmanuel Charles Edwards: Founder of the Bobo Ashanti Order in 1958.

Global North: The term "Global North" correlates with the Western world and refers to the more economically developed and industrialized countries located primarily in the northern hemisphere. It is often used in contrast to the Global South, which refers to less developed or developing countries located primarily in the southern hemisphere.

Haile Selassie (1892-1975)**:** Former emperor of Ethiopia from 1930 to 1970, and central to the belief of Rastafarianism.

Livity: the Rastafarian concept of righteous, ever living. Its essence is the realization that an energy or life-force, conferred by Almighty Jah (God), exists.

"Mansions"/Houses/Branches: An umbrella word for the numerous Rastafari movements that includes the Bobo Ashanti, the Niyabinghi, and the twelve tribes of Israel.

Marcus Garvey: Jamaican political activist, ideologically a Black Nationalist and Pan-Africanist. His ideas came to be referred as Garveyism.

Marijuana: A psychoactive drug from the cannabis plant used for medical or recreational purposes.

Prophet Gad Carrington: Founder of the 12 tribes of Israel in 1968.

Pan Africanism: Emerged in the late 19th and early 20th centuries in response to the subjugation and exploitation of Africans by European powers. It gained momentum as a response to the racial discrimination and segregation faced by African people both within Africa and in the diaspora.

Rastas: A term for individuals who identify with the Rastafarian religion.

Rastafarianism: A religious movement that began in Jamaica in the 1930s

Reggae: A popular music genre that originated in Jamaica in the late 1960s. It is characterized by its distinctive rhythm, relaxed and offbeat sound, and socially conscious lyrics.

The Pinnacle: The first Rastafarian village in Jamaica established by Leonard Howell.

Wailing Souls: Reggae group from Jamaica that popularized Rastafari through its music.

Quotations from Marcus Garvey

We are going to emancipate ourselves from mental slavery because whilst others might free the body, none but ourselves can free the mind. Mind is your only ruler, sovereign. The man who is not able to develop and use his mind is bound to be the slave of the other man who uses his mind.

A people without the knowledge of their past history, origin and culture is like a tree without roots.

If you have no confidence in self, you are twice defeated in the race of life.

A race that is solely dependent upon another for economic existence sooner or later dies. As we have in the past been living upon the mercies shown by others, and by the chances obtainable, and have suffered there from, so we will in the future suffer if an effort is not made now to adjust our own affairs.

The thing to do is to get organized; keep separated and you will be exploited, you will be robbed, you will be killed. Get organized and you will compel the world to respect you.

No one knows when the hour of Africa's redemption cometh. It is in the wind. It is coming. One day, like a storm, it will be here.

Climb ye the heights of liberty and cease not in well doing until you have planted the banner of the Red, the Black and the Green on the hilltops of Africa.

Timeline

1930: Emperor Haile Selassie I is crowned in Ethiopia. His coronation is a pivotal event for the Rastafari movement, as many Rastafarians believe he is the messiah and fulfillment of biblical prophecies.

1930s-1940s: Leonard Howell, considered one of the early Rastafari leaders, begins spreading the movement's teachings in Jamaica. He emphasizes the repatriation of black people to Africa, the rejection of Western culture, and the worship of Emperor Haile Selassie.

1940s: Rastafarianism faces opposition and persecution from Jamaican authorities due to its rejection of colonial and societal norms. Many Rastafarians are arrested and their dreadlocked appearance is often misunderstood or stigmatized, YBF also emerges.

1950s: The Rastafari movement gains visibility through the emergence of reggae music, particularly with artists like Bob Marley, Peter Tosh, and Bunny Wailer. These musicians incorporate Rastafarian themes into their lyrics, helping to popularize the movement's messages and philosophy.

1966: Emperor Haile Selassie I visits Jamaica, which is seen as a significant event for the Rastafari movement. This further legitimizes the movement's beliefs and contributes to its growth.

Late 1960s-early 1970s: The "Back to Africa" movement gains momentum among Rastafarians. Many Rastafarians begin to see repatriation to Africa, particularly Ethiopia, as a way to escape the racism and oppression they face in the Western world.

1981: Bob Marley, one of the most famous Rastafarian musicians, passes away. His music and advocacy continue to have a profound impact on the Rastafari movement and its global recognition.

1990s: The Rastafari movement continues to grow internationally, with followers in various countries around the world. The movement's cultural influence is also seen in fashion, art, and literature.

2000s: The Rastafari movement faces challenges of identity and interpretation as it becomes more diverse and spreads to different cultures and regions.

Present: Rastafarianism remains an important cultural and religious movement, advocating for social justice, equality, and African identity. Its influence can still be seen in various aspects of global culture, and its messages continue to resonate with people seeking empowerment and spiritual connection.

It's important to note that the Rastafari movement is diverse and decentralized, with different branches and interpretations of its beliefs. This timeline provides a general overview, but there are many variations and developments within the movement that are not captured here.

Further Reading

Rasta and Resistance: From Marcus Garvey to Walter Rodney. Horace Campbell, 1987.

Rastafari: A Very Short Introduction, Ennis Barrington Edmonds, 2012.

Becoming Rasta: Origins of Rastafari Identity in Jamaica. Charles Price, 2009.

Chanting Down Babylon: The Rastafari Reader. Nathaniel Samuel Murrell, 1998.

The Rastafarians. Leonard E. Barrett Sr, 1977.

Selected Writings and Speeches of Marcus Garvey. Marcus Garvey, 2004.

Rastafari: Roots and Ideology (Utopianism and Communitarianism). Barry Chevannes, 1994.

My Life and Ethiopia's Progress: The Autobiography of Emperor Haile Selassie I Volume One: 1892-1937.

The Kebra Nagast: Introduction: V. Summary of the Contents of the Kĕbra Nagast. (n.d.). Sacred-Texts.com. Retrieved 12 August 2023, from https://sacred-texts.com/afr/kn/kn008.htm

Visions of Zion: Ethiopians and Rastafari in the Search for the Promised Land. Eric Macleod.

The First Rasta: Leonard Howell and the Rise of Rastafarianism. Hélène Lee.

Dread Talk: The Language of the Rastafari. Velma Pollard.

Bibliography

Books

Bedasse, M. A. (2017). Jah Kingdom: Rastafarians, Tanzania, and Pan-Africanism in the Age of Decolonization. Chapel Hill, The University of North Carolina Press

Burgess, V. (2007). Indian Influences on Rastafarianism [Thesis Indian Influences on Rastafarianism]. The Ohio State University. Department of Comparative Studies Honors Theses

Campbell, H. (1987). Rasta and Resistance. New Jersey, Africa World Press, Inc.

Edmonds, E. B. (2002). Rastafari: From Outcasts to Culture Bearers. New York, Oxford University Press

Garvey, M. M. (1986). Philosophy and Opinions of Marcus Garvey. USA, Majority Press

Linden, I. (1997). Liberation Theology. London, CIIR

Prince, C. (2009). Becoming Rasta: Origins of Rastafari Identity in Jamaica. NYU Press

Journal articles

Alleyne, M. (1998). Babylon Makes the Rules: The Politics of Reggae Crossover. *Social and Economic Studies,* 47(1), 65–77. https://www.jstor.org/stable/27866166

adst.org. (2016). Anatomy of an Overthrow: How an African Leader was Toppled – Association for Diplomatic Studies & Training. [online] Available at: https://adst.org/2016/10/anatomy-overthrow-revered-African-leader-toppled [Accessed 27 Sept. 2023]

Barnett, M. (2005). The many faces of Rasta: Doctrinal Diversity within the Rastafari Movement. Caribbean Quarterly, 51(2), 67-78.https://www.jstor.org/stable/40654506?origin=JSTOR-pdf

Chawane, M. H. (2014). The Rastafarian movement in South Africa: A religion or way of life? *Journal for the Study of Religion,* 27(2), 214–237. http://www.scielo.org.za/scielo.php?script=sci_arttext&pid=S1011-7601201400020001

Newspaper articles

Autodidacy 17. (31 August 2017). *Marcus Mosiah Garvey: Emancipate your African mind!* New York Amsterdam News. https://amsterdamnews.com/news/2017/08/31/marcus-mosiah-garvey-emancipate-your-african-mind

Demby, G. (13 May 2015). *I'm From Philly. 30 Years Later, I'm Still Trying To Make Sense Of The MOVE Bombing.* NPR.org. https://content.time.com/time/magazine/article/0,9171,141842,00.htm

The Star. (2020). *A glimpse into Rastafarianism in Kenya, its history.* [online] Available at: https://www.the-star.co.ke/sasa/lifestyle/2020-06-12-a-glimpse-into- rastafarianism-in-kenya-its-history/.

www.pd.co.ke. (2020). *Rastafarian movement in Kenya mourns its fallen leader – Moses Mbugua.* [online] Available at: https://www.pd.co.ke/news/rastafarian-movement-in-kenya-mourns-its-fallen-leader-moses-mbugua-37673/.

The Guardian. (2020). *Chuck Sims Africa freed: final jailed Move 9 member released from prison*, 7 February, Pilkington, E.

Websites

Africa at LSE. (2019). *The romantic rewriting of Haile Selassie's legacy must stop.* [online] Available at: https://blogs.lse.ac.uk/africaatlse/2019/02/04/the-romantic-rewriting-of-haile-selassies-legacy-must-stop/.

A-Z Quotes. (2015). *TOP 25 QUOTES BY MARCUS GARVEY (of 123)* | A-Z Quotes. [online] Available at: https://www.azquotes.com/author/5371-Marcus_Garvey.

Brotherhood In Islam. (9 February 2022). www.al-Islam.org. https://www.al-islam.org/islamic-moral-system-tafsir-commentary-surah-al-hujarat-49-jafar subhani/brotherhood-islam

Black History Month 2023. (2008). *Haile Selassie – King, God or Redeemer?* [online] Available at: https://www.blackhistorymonth.org.uk/article/section/bhm-he%20roes/haile-selassie-king-god-or-redeemer/ [Accessed 3 Oct. 2023].

Bean, B. (2014). *'I-And-I Vibration': Word, Sound, and Power in Rastafari Music and Reasoning.* mdsoar.org. [online] doi: https://doi.org/10.13016/M2VJ4F.

Contributors (2014). *Terrorists or a MOVEment? Never Forget May 13th,1985.* [online] The Black Youth Project. Available at: https://blackyouthproject.com/terrorists-or-a-movement-never-forget-may-13th1985 [Accessed 27 Sep. 2023].

Coursehero.com. (2023). Available at: https://www.coursehero.com/file/23635170/Rafarianism [Accessed 27 Sept. 2023].

Club, A.N.Z.R. (2023). *Why do Rastas use the Star of David?* [online] www.newzealandrabbitclub.net. Available at: https://www.newzealandrabbitclub.net/why-do-rastas-use-the-star-of-david/

Daniels, V. (2020, December 11). *How Buddhism Teaches us to Un-Learn the Mindset of Materialism.* Medium. https://medium.com/mind-cafe/how-buddhism-teaches-us-to-un-learn-the-mindset-of-materialism-81e1f2b8afa2

Encyclopedia Britannica. (n.d.). sawm | *Religion, Meaning, Reasons, & Importance.* [online] Available at: https://www.britannica.com/topic/sawm

Eschert, R (2023). Uvm.edu. (2023). Available at: https://www.uvm.edu/~debate/dreadlibrary/eschert.html.

Fagan, C. (2021). *The history of Queen Nyabinghi, Shamanic Priestess of East Africa.* [online] AfricaOTR. Available at: https://africaotr.com/the-history-of-queen-nyabinghi-shamanic-priestess-of-east-africa/

History.com Editors. (2018, August 21). *Rastafarianism.* HISTORY; A&E Television Networks. https://www.history.com/topics/religion/history-of-rastafarianism

History.com Editors (2017). *Hinduism.* [online] History. Available at: https://www.history.com/topics/religion/hinduism.

Jamaica Observer. (2015). *Reliving one of Jamaica's bloodiest events — the tragedy at Coral Gardens.* [online] Available at: https://www.jamaicaobserver.com/%20 news/reliving-one-of-jamaicas-bloodiest-events-the-tragedy-at-coral-gardens/ [Accessed 27 Sept. 2023].

Musodza, M. (2015). *The Ties That Bind: Reggae, Rastafari, Judaism and Israel.* [online] blogs.timesofisrael.com. Available at: https://blogs.timesofisrael.com/the-ties-that-bind-reggae-rastafari-judaism-and-israel/.

Rahula, W. S. (2015). *The Noble Eightfold Path: Meaning and Practice. Tricycle:* The Buddhist Review; Tricycle. https://tricycle.org/magazine/noble-eightfold-path/

YADA, R. (n.d.). *The Incient Nyahbinghi Order*: [Review of The Incient Nyahbinghi Order]. Durban, Isalem Publications

Symbol Sage. (2021). *List of Rastafarian Symbols and Their Meaning.* [online] Available at: https://symbolsage.com/rastafarian-symbols-list-meaning/.

Sacred-texts.com. (n.d.). *The Kebra Nagast: Introduction: V. Summary of the Contents of the Kĕbra Nagast.* [online] Available at: https://sacred-texts.com/afr/kn/kn008.htm.

www.marxists.org. (2006). *The Targeting of Walter Rodney* | Solidarity. [online] Available at: https://www.marxists.org/history/etol/newspape/atc/136.html.

www.tozion.org. (n.d.). *The Sabbath * Rastafari * ToZion.org *.* [online] Available at: https://www.tozion.org/Rastafari-Sabbath.html [Accessed 12 Aug. 2023]